THE WAR IN ME

THE WAR IN ME

Finding Resolution to Injustices served by
Society, Relationships as well as Ourselves

*The Accounts of a British-Afghan
Mother and Daughter*

BY NILAB AZIMI

First paperback edition 2023

Book design by Publishing Push

978-1-80541-069-0 (paperback)
978-1-80541-070-6 (ebook)

Contents

Introduction

My name is Nilab, and I live in London with my mum. I'm originally from Kabul, Afghanistan, a war-torn country that Mum and
I fled when I was a young child. I am an only child, though I come
from quite a large extended family, consisting of three uncles, six
aunties, cousins as well as seconds cousins, all of whom we had to
leave behind due to the volatile situation in Afghanistan. My mum
is now my only family.

Prior to moving to the UK, I spent a few years living in New
Delhi, India, where I began to appreciate diversity and differences
in culture, ways of life, experiences, as well as the different struggles
people face. As time went on and I became older, I further witnessed
the many battles people are likely to be confronted with.

I have wanted to write about my mum's life for as long as I can
remember, to put into words what my mum has been through,
though felt held back by self-doubt. Just as my mum felt weighed
down by different life events, I too sensed pressure, pressure to write
in such a way which was acknowledging and validating of my mum's
reality. Furthermore, looking back, it is possible that there were also
parts of me which wanted to protect my mum from some of the
things she has fought so hard to battle with and overcome. I believe

now is the right time, as I am writing this as an adult who has also experienced certain struggles and challenges and having engaged in my own self-reflection.

For the first time, through this book, I have expressed certain feelings around the lessons life has taught me. I also want to show readers that there is richness and wisdom created by what life presents, making a person multi-faceted: strong yet vulnerable; rich and poor; young and old.

I have had all kinds of responses from other people when I have disclosed that I am originally from Afghanistan, which has led me to have mixed feelings regarding talking about my origins. On the one hand, I don't want to be made to feel a certain way depending on the other person's response. On the other hand, I believe telling a person allows us to connect and for them to develop a deeper appreciation of who I am.

Over the years I have encountered substantial difficulty connecting with what it really means to be both Afghan and British. Maybe my take on my identity and life would have been different if I continued to live in Kabul, particularly as I imagine life would have panned out differently. Nonetheless, by not having the possibility to experience what could have been, I have tried to connect with what that has been like for me. This has involved me finding other ways in connecting with society, relationships, and myself.

Gratitude is something which I have been able to develop a deep connection with, which was something promoted in the strong relationship I have with my mum. Gratitude has been a major source of strength, courage, and hope for both my mum and I. I have seen how Mum has expressed gratitude for what she has, even when events brought difficulty.

My mum learned about gratitude from her father, who was a righteous and steadfast person with a strong faith. He would tell my mum about the people he had encountered who were in compromised situations and circumstances, yet he could also see the hope and desire in them to persevere and not give up on themselves and life.

I would be very surprised if readers had heard of me prior to discovering this book, as this is the first time I am writing in such a way. Writing, however, has played a key part in my life, as I have used it to give expression to the many things I have encountered. It has been a way for me to reflect on and acknowledge hardships and setbacks, as well as triumphs. From the time I was able to read, I remember feeling enthralled by the detail and language of different books. I recall my delight when a dedicated time was given to reading when I was at school, where there was a broad collection of books which I would eagerly explore. My mum also encouraged me to enrich and expand my vision of the world through books and develop my understanding of the meaning behind words.

The title of this book, "The War in Me", I believe captures the battles I have witnessed and endured. Alongside acknowledging what my mum and I have been at war with, my intention was to also acknowledge the different struggles we all confront, albeit in different ways and degrees. As I embarked on and engaged in the writing process, I began to uncover more things, recognising the various conflicts, struggles, and challenges both my mum and I had experienced. The more I expressed and created space for expression regarding different events and experiences, the more I felt able and determined to write in different ways, which led to me connecting with the poet in me. Therefore, the book also gave me the opportunity to write poetry as a way of relating to and connecting with myself and others. My intention has been to inspire those reading this book to develop ways of relating to themselves and their experiences, acknowledging and expressing how they truly want to be.

By becoming more aware of moments of distress and adversity, I have striven to show the vulnerability that is part of existence and broaden understanding of how vulnerability can be a source of curiosity, wisdom, and compassion, enabling us to navigate responsively in the world. By reframing my view of what it means to be vulnerable, I have begun to see the risks I have taken, the challenges I have set myself, and the many strides I have made, all of which have taken me to places I had never even imagined. The beliefs, views, perceptions, and attitudes we form undoubtedly inform the positions we take. Even though they can offer meaning and enhance understanding, we may at times find ourselves captive or held back by what we are saying and communicating to ourselves through them. Some of the beliefs, views, and perceptions I held towards myself without doubt created major roadblocks, to the point that I had given up the possibility of ever writing anything like this. What cleared the blockage? It was a dream. Yes, I had a dream whilst sleeping where I vividly saw a book, this book, coming into formation even seeing its title! It was as if a part of me was communicating that I have it in me to write in such a way. I do tend to have quite vivid dreams which can feel very real, and I had a strong desire to turn this dream into reality. Even after having dreamt about writing this book, I could not have seen myself taking on such a task. It has been my mum who has always been my source of inspiration and support. She has enabled me to challenge myself and by doing so, face my deepest anxieties. My mum has been with me throughout the journey and has taught me about the importance of picking yourself up from setbacks. In many ways, my mum's life story has given me courage and determination even though there were occasions I considered omitting certain experiences because of the feelings attached to them. I did not want to expose my mum or myself to any more emotional hurt and demolish the layers of protection that we had built up.

As well as providing accounts of mine and my mum's lives, the book also highlights knowledge and wisdom gained from different experiences and life lessons contributing to who and how I am. Sharing in this book my experiences and engagement in the field of mental health is intended to provide ideas, resources, and practices readers may find helpful in promoting wellbeing.

I imagine a person picking up this book and thinking, 'Why would I want to read about someone's life story, particularly if I don't know them?' It's true, the reality is that we tend to be drawn to people we have a connection with, and as I do not see myself as a publicly recognisable figure, I wondered who would be interested, thinking, 'I'm just an ordinary person.' I may be an ordinary person but some of the things I have encountered have been anything but ordinary. I believe life is about navigating between the good and the not so good, and through the process of writing I could imagine I was in some way connecting with other people and making them feel heard. I know for example, that most people have experienced some kind of loss. It could be the loss of someone through death, separation or estrangement, or the loss of livelihood, health, identity, and freedom. My mum and I have definitely encountered such losses which I will be sharing with you, the reader.

Writing this book has created different feelings in me as it involved taking myself to times and places, some of which were nostalgic and some bringing about different degrees of emotional pain. In addition, I was aware of experiencing internal conflict: pausing, reading back, and questioning whether the book was going to be good enough. 'Will other people get me? Will my experiences resonate with other people? Have I understood different people when I have referred to what difficult experiences can lead to as well as what more helpful responses towards ourselves might be?' There are parts of the book which I had previously decided to write about and there were other parts which came about as I engaged in the writing. It was as if I needed to take myself on the journey first before inviting the reader along.

Speaking of journeys, my professional journey has offered me a rich and varied experience as I have been able to meet, work with, and get to know individuals from diverse backgrounds and walks of life. My engagement with academia as well as in the field of mental health, having worked across a number of settings, has taught me a great deal giving me the ability to utilise a variety of knowledge and skills. To this day I remember the words one of my first supervisors said to me, which were, 'No matter how much training and skills you have, leave them at the door when you enter the room with another person.' I remember initially finding the advice unsettling and even questioned why I had dedicated so much of my time, energy, and focus on academia. However, as I progressed in my professional life, these words began to make more sense and became a source of reassurance. For me, the greatest learning happened and continues to happen during my interactions with others, as I am understanding more and more how emotional pain and distress is inevitable, but the lesson is in how we respond to and navigate this. I have been amazed listening to other people's stories, what they have been battling with as well as the things they have triumphed over. When it comes to listening, I strive to listen, with my ears, eyes, mind, heart, and body. I want to attune to what a person is expressing in the way they can and need to. I see myself as very fortunate to be a part of an individual's journey, as I know how important and influential others have been in my own personal journey. The people in my life have not only played different roles but have also influenced some of the decisions and courses of action I have taken. I am aware that not everyone has supportive people in their lives and how important it is to develop different sources of support and positive influence. From the various professional roles I have taken on, I can really see the significance of being a supportive and encouraging person for others as well as ourselves. Of course, there are bound to be hurdles along the way which may take many forms, but so long as we find the strength and courage to help ourselves get over, through or around them, this in itself is a commitment and investment in ourselves.

I strongly believe experiences, insight, knowledge, and wisdom need to be shared and passed on, so allow me to do that with you.

I hope what I have written conveys to the reader how every person's experience is valid and worthy of being expressed. Mine and my mum's stories tell of how we have at times been limited in our ability to flourish and be the people we want to be. Developing a commitment and investment in ourselves is what can push us through such limitations. I hope through the accounts of mine and my mum's lives, the reader can see how they too can rise and flourish in the way they want.

Having written about the importance of self-acceptance and self-compassion, I believe it is these ways of relating to ourselves which can help create new opportunities and possibilities.

CHAPTER 1

I can't wait to meet you!

'Here she is!' said the doctor to an exhausted Mum after thirteen hours of labour and contractions every five minutes. Held up before Mum was a baby, which for the first time was alive. You could say it was a miracle: Mum had finally become a mother after a miscarriage and four still births, having put her health and life on the line, being bed-bound for the final six months, and in Berlin, Germany, a foreign country where she was far from family and loved ones.

'I want to try even if it costs me my life!' is what Mum said to concerned others. What can I say, Mum is someone who strives to get what she wants, and having a child was what she deeply desired and yearned for.

'Don't take her away!' Mum cried loudly as I was about to be taken to another room. 'Is she OK?' There was an overwhelming sense of panic in her voice at this point. It was nothing serious, I had developed jaundice and needed to be kept in an incubator.

'She's fine,' said staff reassuringly, and after three days Mum was able to hold me for the first time.

'I'm a mother, she is mine.' Mum was in a state of utter disbelief and could not wait to show me to the only family she had in Berlin, my uncle and his wife. They were living in Berlin as my uncle worked there as an ambassador and had their own preoccupations especially as they had a baby two months previously. 'She's tiny! How can I look after her?'

Despite Mum having long prepared for motherhood, she had a lot of self-doubt and constant fear that something awful would happen to me. This was in light of the difficulties she experienced with previous pregnancies leading to her feeling incapable of being able to protect and look after a baby.

'Don't you want to see your daughter?' asked my uncle in sheer frustration when Dad arrived from Kabul to take Mum and I home.

'She's nice,' Dad remarked, as he ever so lightly touched my cheek.

A bit about my dad. He came from a family of five sisters and two brothers, though both his brothers had passed away, leaving him the only son. His mother was someone who looked after the children whilst his father was occupied with business affairs, and his parents did not appear to have had a loving relationship. His father was so engrossed in his work, which involved him spending significant periods of time abroad, that he saw his dad for the first time when he was five. The father-son relationship that they went on to have was one that was focused on work. Dad pretty much had his career mapped out, which was to continue the different busi-nesses his father had established. When it came to Dad's relationship with Mum, he had been relentless in gaining her trust and love, which took a number of years given Mum's concerns around Dad's past. Dad had been quite careless in his younger years, and ended up getting a woman pregnant with whom he had no relationship. After discovering that he had gotten the woman pregnant, he fled the country to start a new life elsewhere to avoid responsibility. The woman's family however, were adamant that they would find Dad and bring him back to Kabul and get him to marry their daughter. 'It was an accident, and I was very young,' was Dad's explanation to Mum after she discovered from someone else about Dad having a child.

Now, a little about Mum. Mum is the youngest of nine children, six girls and three boys, and was sweet and loveable from a young age. Mum's father, whom she had a very close relationship with, passed away when she was eleven, and her mother, whom she also had a very loving relationship with, passed away when Mum was in her early twenties and six months after she had married Dad. Grandma's death was quite sudden and traumatic and my eldest aunty Khala Shahgul stepped in, becoming a source of comfort and support for Mum.

When mum returned home with me, family and loved ones could not have been any more welcoming. Most of them knew how much Mum wanted to have a child and witnessed the harrowing events around her losses; three girls and two boys (the two before me were twins; a boy and a girl). Every time Mum got close to becoming a mother, the further she felt she was getting. It is something which still haunts her to this day, that she was not able to nurture, and watch grow the children she lost. Khlala Shahgul was the strongest support for Mum, being a mother to a childless mother. It was Khala Shahgul who was the most delighted and was eagerly waiting for Mum and I to arrive. Khala Shahgul was the second person after Mum who I experienced an abundance of love from.

'Welcome home!' 'You're a mother!' cried family.

'Yes, I am!' exclaimed Mum, her eyes filled with tears of joy and triumph.

'Is the wall finished yet?' asked Mum, speaking to her nephew who was putting up decorations for my first birthday in Kabul.

'Almost done!' he replied, with intense excitement in his voice.

'And are the musicians on their way?' Mum asked another nephew, who was also going to be performing.

'Yes, they are!' he said.

I will never forget my birthdays, even the very early ones. They were grand and extravagant, and Mum would go to great lengths planning and preparing to make them an enjoyable and positively immersive experience for all. I remember family and friends eagerly waiting for my birthdays to arrive and even with the passing of time they would speak of them with delight. I would say they were some of the best moments of my life.

As my birthdays showed, Mum always wanted the best for me. She wanted me to have a good upbringing and education, which was something she sacrificed for herself to be with Dad. Mum had high academic and career aspirations for herself and had even begun attending a university in Kabul studying English and Psychology, which were two of her favourite subjects. Mum stopped going after three days. Why? Because of Dad.

'I saw how guys were looking at you as I dropped you off,' he remarked.

'I didn't notice,' replied Mum.

'What's the point? You don't need to go. It's not like you will need to work. You will have all the money you need. It's either me or university,' was Dad's ultimatum. It was a time when Mum was madly in love with him and just as she imagined Dad being prepared to do anything for her, she was also prepared to do anything for him, believing that he would be supportive in other aspects. This was a time when Mum felt deeply conflicted. On her side of the family, education was something highly regarded and where there was high academic potential. All three of Mum's brothers and a few other family members had been awarded international scholarships due to having academically excelled, with one of Mum's brother's progressing to attaining professorship status.

Mum could see her academic potential and so could her family and growing up, she was greatly supported by her brothers. If only the encouragement and support also came from Dad.

Dad's family on the other hand, was involved in several businesses, both domestic and international, and education was not so high on the agenda. Dad was able to establish himself on a professional level as a businessman but over time failed to do so as a partner and a father.

Mum however strived immensely to establish herself as a wife and mother. It was apparent even before I came into this world that Mum had infinite love for me. During her pregnancy, she would talk lovingly and endearingly to me about all the things she was prepared to do for me. Our deep bond developed whilst Mum was in hospital and alone for most of her pregnancy. Just like Mum was prepared to provide me with everything I needed, you could say I was also able to provide for her. Having me with her she was able to express the myriad of intentions, hopes, as well as emotions she was experiencing.

Becoming a mother informed a big part of Mum's identity and created a sense of purpose for her. Prior to me being in Mum's life the numerous setbacks she encountered filled her with anguish and a sense of hopelessness. It led to her questioning her existence and whether there was any point in her living a life where she was constantly battling.

Mum's relationship with Dad was one such battle which created tension between her and some family members. 'I'm telling you, he will do the same as he did to the first one. He will leave you with a baby!' Mum's brother said with contempt, but I believe Mum was intent on proving how Dad had changed his ways and that he was invested in their relationship.

Over the years, Mum and Dad's relationship did develop complexities, which was not helped by Dad nearly always being away on business leaving Mum spending long periods of time on her own. Dad became less and less available; even when he was physically around, he would be less attentive and emotionally distant, and would subject Mum to harsh words and criticism. This was in stark contrast to how he was previously, showering Mum with love and affection and appearing to be extremely invested and committed to the relationship.

CHAPTER 2

Finding connection

'Do you want some of mine?' I asked a friend at nursery as I intriguingly looked at what they had for lunch. 'OK!' she replied.

I remember sharing and having all kinds of new and exciting things to eat after Mum and I had temporarily moved to New Delhi, India, as the situation in Kabul had deteriorated. We had rented a ground floor property located in a sought-after area where Mum and I began forming friendships and integrating in society. This was my first time in India but not Mum's, as she had previously travelled there for medical treatment before I was born, spending almost a year in a small place on her own. I can imagine how it must have been difficult for Mum leaving family again to go to a foreign country.

Mum made sure I went to the best nursery in the area and later to an American school so that I could also learn English. From what I now know, Mum was very happy for me to go to nursery and school yet also felt extremely anxious as it involved separation, and she worried about whether I would be ok.

When I became older, Mum told me about my first day at nursery and how she had waited outside the whole time, informing the staff that she would be around in case I became distressed. To her surprise I was very content and even began making friends. This was just one of the many instances where Mum was there to make sure I was ok. I would like to have said that Dad was also there for me, but far from it. Looking back, I believe Mum was overcompensating for Dad not being there. Mum was Mum and Dad, and all that was in between.

Despite being in a country where Mum and I did not have any family, she made sure we had positive relationships, opportunities, and experiences. I distinctly remember the colourful and playful Diwali celebrations, going to extravagant weddings and ceremonies, and wearing beautifully custom-made Indian attire. I can truly say I felt part of a community and I was also beginning to connect with my faith. Being a Muslim, I remember going to grand mosques and saw Mum engaging in charitable acts, such as buying food tokens for the poor. What's more is that India also provided me with the foundations for my academic pursuits. With Mum's support and encouragement, I was very enthused, engaged, and committed towards my learning. In addition, Mum arranged private tuition to push me to achieve my academic potential. This was Mum's way of giving me what she deeply wanted after her own academic pursuits were cut short. I was learning so much and in a multitude of ways, for which I will always be grateful to Mum.

As well as learning about the value of education, living in New Delhi over a two-year period taught me about the importance of treating everyone with respect and kindness, and the value of friends and community.

With the situation in Afghanistan appearing to settle somewhat we returned to Kabul, and it was great being reunited with family and loved ones. Dad continued spending significant periods of time away on business and being preoccupied with his work, whereas I was spending more time with Mum and her side of the family.

Mum had desperately tried to prevent me being an only child, yet given the difficulties with her pregnancies, she always sought to provide me with opportunities to socialise and connect with other children. I was the youngest child and remember cousins and second cousins being loving and attentive towards me. I also remember Mum having close family friends, whose children I enjoyed spending time with. One family friend in particular always comes to mind, even to this day, as I was always very excited and happy when we would visit them. Whenever I used to go to this family friend's house I felt as if I had three older brothers. I loved going there so much that I would insist on staying overnight. The political situation in Kabul at the time was such that an evening curfew was imposed whereby no one was allowed to be out after a certain time. This was even more reason for me to spend more time with such lovely and warm people. In the mornings I recall being woken up by the wonderful smell of freshly fried eggs. The family had a chicken farm which I would regularly explore and where one day they surprised me with twenty-five chicks. The garden of this family friend had an assortment of trees, and I was particularly fascinated by the pistachio tree with bright green and pink hues. At the other end of the garden was a huge tree which would blossom with white flowers, and a bit like "The Secret Garden", if you went further on into the garden, there was another house where the in-laws lived, who were also very nice people.

CHAPTER 3

Saying goodbye

We celebrated my sixth birthday in Kabul. At that point we had moved into a much smaller place which we were renting. The family home and other properties had been sold and the money shared amongst Dad's family, who had begun to immigrate to the US.

The situation in Kabul had worsened to the point where war was imminent, and we were truly beginning to fear for our safety. We never imagined having to leave Kabul forever. Kabul was my home, Mum's home, her family's home, and the home of previous generations. It was where we ultimately belonged, and it was going to be an immense loss. The biggest loss was having to leave our loved ones, as we did not know when or if we would see them again. It was also a loss of the life we were no longer able to have, and we were going to immigrate to a country where life would be very different. Although we would have more safety, we would not have the lifestyle and the luxuries we had up to that point. We were going to become refugees, asking for instead of being in control of what we could have, and even then, it would not amount to what we could have had in pre-war Afghanistan.

In Afghanistan we were quite well established and had a good reputation but being in another country, we felt we had to build this from scratch. What will this country offer? Looking back, I cannot fully recall what I was thinking and feeling but do hold strong emotions towards saying goodbye to everyone and everything in Afghanistan. It was one of the most heart-breaking moments of my life. I also remember Mum giving her possessions, particularly jewellery and other monetary high-value items to family particularly, my aunty Khala Shahgul, who had become more like a grandmother to me and a mother to Mum. In one way this gesture was to show Mum's appreciation for the love, care, and support as well as the significant role people like my aunty had in her life. It was also a symbolic gesture which I believe made Mum feel that there would always be a connection between them.

In my mind I often revisit beautiful moments and significant experiences of my life in Kabul which I find deeply captivating and heart-warming. Mum had so much more that she was saying goodbye to, though she has taken a lot from Afghanistan and brought to the UK: her culture, faith, and the positive relationships and memories which were made there.

Where were we leaving Kabul behind for? It was a place Dad, his father and grandfather had professional connections with and somewhere Mum would eagerly wait for Dad to return from following long business trips. The place was London. Two of Mum's school friends had started a new life there so Mum felt reassured that she knew a few people there who she would be reunited with. For Mum, coming with hardly anything except a few suitcases in many ways reminded her of travelling to Germany and India, both trips also being about safety and preserving life, only this time it was going to be for an unknown period of time. Striving to create safety and preserve life was something Mum had been doing for a long time. Having tried hard to keep safe and preserve the lives of the children she had lost, Mum was prepared to do anything and everything to keep me alive, safe, and raise me in such a way that I was able to flourish.

For the first two weeks in London, we stayed with one of Mum's school friends. Even though we arrived in London with just a few suitcases, Mum had packed gifts for the people she would see. I cannot say our stay at the friend's house was comfortable, after all it was their house, and they had their own way of running it. We would get woken up in the early hours of the morning by the family's regimented cleaning routine. Dad was also regularly asked by the family whether he had found us a place to stay. After the two weeks we felt we had outdone our stay, and Mum's other family friend invited us to stay with them.

We spent two months staying with this family friend, which on the whole was a positive experience, particularly as I became friends with the children and felt very welcome and part of the family. Our stay was as good for them as it was for us in that Mum, despite having her own battles, helped the friend restore her marital relationship.

During our time at this friend's place, we were contacted by the government about accommodation. Mum and I were dismayed when we visited the place, which was a bedsit. It was a very confined space: just one room to eat and sleep in, with a shared toilet and bathroom. It was also then that Dad dropped the bombshell that he was going to the US to care for his dad, whose health was deteriorating. He expressed that as the only son, he needed to be there for his dad and could not say when he would return. It was very unsettling for Mum and I, not having any certainty over how long we would stay in such a place, or our future.

Mum now had to assume even more responsibility for our lives as we struggled to integrate into a very different society, at a time when there was not as much ethnic and cultural diversity. Mum had almost no external support, but her faith and determination in wanting the best for me superseded the reality we were met with. Despite setbacks and challenges, Mum was determined to make things work. She was prepared to fight with all her might, even though we had the bare minimum, not only when it came to possessions and our living situation but also regarding social and cultural connections.

CHAPTER 4

Striving to belong

I vividly remember feeling like an outsider and very disconnected, having so many sources of comfort and connection removed. In some ways I still feel that way to this day, as I mourn over the losses I have encountered over the years. Mum and I found ourselves in an overwhelming situation. How could we obtain what we needed? With Dad away and not offering much support, the government became the provider of shelter, education, healthcare, and other resources. The government became a substitute partner to Mum and a substitute father to me.

Mum and I had to stay in the bedsit for almost a year before being provided with a flat above a high street shop. This new place was definitely bigger than the bedsit and there were more rooms, as well as a small garden at the back. It was somewhere we could call home for the time being, yet it had an eerie feel to it. Despite it being much bigger, there was an emptiness and starkness to the place. During the day you could see how it was part of a busy high street with people around and vehicles travelling past, but when the evening came and the shops and businesses closed, it felt as if the flat was also closing in on us. We had no neighbours and no one to contact, no one to see or speak to. I remember Mum's bedroom being right at the end of the flat, and it was very cold and gloomy, which was not conducive to a good night's sleep. In fact, it was a place where Mum's anxiety heightened and there was no way she could rest. It was then Mum started taking medication to help alleviate the impact of uprooting her life and being somewhere which felt far from the emotional safety she needed.

Mum did her best to create a sense of belonging, broadening her social network, forming friendships as well as developing her language skills.

Although she had learnt English in Kabul where she worked as a travel agent, prior to marring Dad, and also spoke English during her time in India, the level of proficiency needed to manage life in the UK was a lot higher. As well as brushing up on her language skills, Mum also wanted to convey her appreciation for being given a life in the UK by offering her time working on a voluntary basis in charity shops. Mum put tremendous effort into making us feel connected and to bring joy and fulfilment into our lives. She was very keen for me not to miss out on social opportunities where I could explore my interests. It was not long before Mum found ballet classes for me, followed by me joining the Brownies and later Guides where I could feel part of a community, have fun, and learn invaluable life skills.

Much like she had done on my birthdays in Kabul and later in New Delhi, Mum went to great lengths in throwing me extravagant birthday parties, even with the little money she had.

Dad remained absent, though Mum made every effort to maintain contact. I do not remember speaking with Dad much and believe even when I did, it was Mum who initiated it.

Mum began to address our living needs and was committed to finding us a permanent home. One of the places we were offered was overlooking a cemetery. This was triggering for Mum given how she had fought so hard to escape the war in Afghanistan and the reality of people being killed there on a daily basis. Mum was adamant in expressing what we needed. 'I want to be able to live somewhere that is close-knit,' she stated to the council. It was extremely difficult being torn apart from loved ones, and Mum was yearning to be part of a community again. Back in Afghanistan, Mum remembers her neighbours being like family, and this was something she was seeking in London.

It took some time before Mum was contacted about a place that resembled what she was looking for. To our surprise, it was located in a place close to the bedsit, but was somewhere we enjoyed walking around, and we could not have been any happier. It was the first time since moving to London where we had neighbours, and we were no longer alone.

Despite living in what appeared to be a peaceful and serene part of London, Mum and I encountered racial abuse and discrimination. On the one hand, we knew we would not have been safe if we had stayed in Kabul, but on the other hand, living in a place where we were experiencing a lack of emotional and psychological safety created a deep sense of anger, frustration, and disillusionment. The reality was we had no one but each other and it was another period of Mum's life where she made every effort to keep me safe.

CHAPTER 5

It's a hard pill to swallow

Over time, the accumulating stresses of life began to take a toll on Mum's health. In many ways her body and mind were saying that what she had endured had been overwhelming and became all consuming. I was unsurprised at how Mum's health had deteriorated though what I am amazed by is how strong she had been and continues to be regardless of her poor health. She is truly inspirational, courageous, and has taught me a lot about persevering and fighting on.

I can recall countless times when Mum's health deteriorated so much that urgent medical attention was required. One of these was when Dad had returned to London for the first time after leaving for the US. At this point Mum had not only assumed all the responsibility for looking after us, but she also wanted to show Dad what she could do for him whilst he was here, with the hope that he might choose to come and live with us in the UK. Up until that point Dad had made it seem he was spending time in the US not only to look after his father in his last days but also to see what opportunities there were, with the intention of creating a better life for us. That first time Dad returned, Mum was so happy that she planned to host a party, inviting everyone she and Dad knew. It was that very day, whilst Mum was preparing for the party, that she collapsed, and an ambulance was called. After undergoing numerous medical examinations, it was discovered that she had developed diabetes.

Further stresses included the calls she received about the passing of family members. She was faced with countless losses, one after another, all of which contributed to Mum developing additional health problems. The phone call I remember the most was when I was around eleven years old. It was from abroad and from someone who Mum did not know very well, expressing condolences for Mum losing two of her sisters. This was news to Mum as our extended family had kept that news from her as they feared she would not be able to bear it. Mum was close to all her siblings, but the two sisters she was closest to were the ones she had discovered were no longer here. To her dismay, Khala Shahgul, the sister who was like a mother, a best friend, a teacher, and a mentor, who Mum had learned so much from, was one of the sisters she had lost. It was traumatic enough having to leave them behind when we left Kabul, when Mum believed that one day she would be reunited with them. Such a permanent loss was something her heart could not take, quite literally.

On that day I remember calling the family doctor who came to examine Mum at home as she had fainted upon hearing the devasting news. The family doctor called for an ambulance and Mum needed to be admitted to hospital where it was discovered that she had developed a narrowing of her heart valve and required surgery.

Mum remained in hospital for some time, and I stayed with a family friend. I remember the anguish I felt not knowing what was going to happen to Mum, the only person who was always there, who kept me safe, and yet there was nothing I could do to keep her safe, feeling defeated. There were moments when doctors performing the surgery also felt defeated, particularly as Mum's heart had stopped for a period of time. Even then, prior to Mum going into cardiac arrest, all she could think of was me, praying to God that I would be safe and well. It was a deeply devastating time for the both of us as we were battling with life in our own ways.

Over the years more and more medical intervention and treatment has been needed regarding Mum's health, which continues to be the case to this day.

I found Dad to be the least empathic person when it came to Mum's health deteriorating. We were once told by a family friend how Dad had said to them that Mum was damaged and there was nothing left in her, which Mum found difficult to believe. If he had really seen Mum in that way, what he really needed to have done was to be there, both for Mum and for me. After all, that was the commitment he had made to Mum when they began their relationship.

I remember a time when Mum did not have money for the bus, and back then fares were a lot cheaper than they are now. However, Mum was determined to support us in every way she possibly could, taking on several jobs and even working seven days a week. I was also determined to support Mum and myself and began working from the age of fourteen. There are people in this world who would do pretty much anything to support their family who I deeply admire. I ask myself, 'Why did Mum not have partner like that? Why did I not have a father like that?!' The thought has left me feeling completely bewildered.

Mum and I do need to be grateful for what Dad has done for us. He got us out of a war-torn country, otherwise 'You and your daughter would have been minced meat,' were Dad's words to Mum. I cannot understand how a person would say such a thing, and in all honesty, it was quite an easy process for him to bring us to the UK given his connections here. The fact is people do acts of kindness if they have the means and opportunity to do so. How could a person change their intentions, ways, and actions to the extent of becoming so unrecognisable? Having once been so besotted with Mum and so invested in their relationship, how could he have become so disregarding, so hostile? Even to this day I have great difficulty making sense of it.

Despite her health being compromised, Mum has always striven to be a source of strength, courage, and hope. If Dad had chosen to stay with us, he could have had this care and support in his life. It could have been that he thought he did not deserve to have such things as growing up he did not receive emotional support from his own dad. This may have led to him questioning whether he was capable of giving and receiving love.

The more Mum lost relationships through physical and emotional wars, the more she ended up forging a relationship with medication. Mum came to understand that medication was going to play a big part in her life as over time it became one of the few things she could depend on. Realising that she would always need to have medical intervention in her life was at the same time met with frustration, resentment, and anxiety around what impact the cocktail of medications was going to have. As well as the loss of her country, loved ones, freedom, livelihood, and dreams, her loss of health is another part of her being that Mum grieves, and is in an ongoing battle with.

CHAPTER 6

Am I good enough?

As I previously mentioned, Mum has always been a responsive and supportive figure in my life, and no matter how big or small my achievements have been, in her eyes each one of them was worthy of praise. Despite Mum not being able to pursue her academic aspirations, she was very encouraging of me pursuing mine. At school, it became apparent that I needed extra support to be able to attain my full academic potential and as soon as Mum realised that she ensured I had all I needed. Mum could only support me so much academically, and so she looked far and wide to identify and provide different types of support whilst ensuring she had the finances to make them accessible to me.

On the contrary, Dad could not have been any less supportive, and I vividly recall a time when he was visiting Mum and I and attempted to teach me some maths. It wasn't long before Dad threw all my books down the stairs and shouted, 'Her head is full of crap, she won't amount to anything!' Those words still haunt me to this day and have greatly impacted my self-confidence, creating doubt about whether I am good enough. Readers may have come across the statement "Sticks and stones may break my bones, but words shall never hurt me," which I wish I could relate to. The cruel words said by Dad, that I am stupid and incapable, I have taken on as my own beliefs towards myself, where I am self-critical as well as holding high expectations of myself.

When I think about whether I am good enough, I also think about whether I deserve to have what I need and want. Dad ensured my half-sister had all she wanted and needed, having taken her and her mum to the US where they were more part of Dad's family than we ever were. Dad had even bought them a house there whilst Mum and I were fighting for the basics.

Looking back, I would say that Mum has overcompensated for what I lacked to get from Dad. She has instilled in me the importance of perseverance and in having trust that I will be able to attain what I desire. I believe Mum also has Dad's harsh words lingering in her mind. From what she has told me, there were countless times where Dad said unkind and even derogatory things to her. One such comment was him having said to Mum, 'Why keep a cow for a glass of milk?!' inferring that he could have quite easily got his sexual needs met with anyone without committing to a relationship. Dad had also said to Mum that he could not differentiate between a duvet cover and Mum's clothing following Mum's weight gain after her pregnancies.

I have come to believe that it was Dad who was not good enough for Mum, nor me for that matter.

Just as they made me become self-critical and doubtful, Dad's criticisms led to Mum becoming extremely self-conscious, judging, and even self-attacking. To this day, Mum tries to present herself in such a way which will not lead to judgement or criticism from others. I have noticed how in relationships Mum always wants to offer the other person as much as she possibly can, which at times comes at a cost, especially if the other person is not as invested as she is. Over the years, I have tried to convey to Mum that she is more than enough and that she only has herself to answer to. I feel a sense of frustration whenever Mum has expressed not believing she has done enough for me and how she also sees herself as a burden to me.

Life has made me realise just how strongly our past can keep us captive and have a hold on us. At the same time, we need to offer ourselves as much kindness, understanding, and support as possible. Just as we encounter different people in our lives, we will also be exposed to different responses. In some ways, it involves accepting that every person comes with their unique history and perception which can have an influence on how they interact with us and that some people will be able to offer more support than others.

Over the years I have become more acknowledging that I am worthy and deserving of love, understanding and support. I certainly have relationships which reflect this, and it has predominantly been in recent years where I have felt more open in being my true self. The brief periods of time Dad did spend with us when I was a child were rife with criticism and ridicule. I recall times when Dad used to mock the way I was in my social interactions and would imitate and belittle me to show me as passive, overwhelmed, or a nervous wreck. Growing up, I anticipated criticism from just about anyone which played out in some of my school years. It has taken a great deal of mental and emotional perseverance and commitment for me to appreciate and value myself.

CHAPTER 7

REALLY getting to know you

Over the years Mum and I have visited various countries and places which began with visiting extended family in different parts of Europe. Prior to obtaining our British citizenship it was a very painstaking process to get a visa involving Mum and I travelling to different embassies across London. Despite not enjoying this process, travelling was something I really enjoyed. I enjoyed being able to see and spend time with loved ones and again feel like the larger family we once were, with traveling also allowing me to see what the world has to offer.

It had been some time since Mum and I had seen Dad as he apparently was unable leave the US. He said to Mum that if we wanted to see him, we could travel to see him. Mum's other intention for going to the US was to see what life there would be like. She had to scrimp and save to find the money for flights and also to buy things for Dad and his family. It was utterly bizarre how we did not have any contact with Dad's family, and yet Mum felt obligated to buy so many gifts, some which were very costly; I remember our suitcases being pretty much filled with them.

Both Mum and I were excited at the prospect of seeing and spending time with Dad and visiting the US for the first time. At that time, we still had our Afghan passports and when Mum told friends that she wanted to travel to the US they were quite discouraging, as back then it was almost impossible to be granted a visa. I recall the day when Mum and I went to the US embassy, feeling excited and eager yet not knowing if it would be a wasted trip. To our surprise, after hours of waiting, and both Mum and I being asked dozens of interrogating questions, our visa application was granted there and then. I enjoyed our time in the U.S, being reunited with cousins I had last seen in Kabul as well as spending time with family I met for the first time. Overall, it was a nice trip.

Another period of time passed, and Dad had other reasons for not being able to come to see us. Mum decided we would make a second trip to the US and this time planning a longer stay as it was the summer holidays. Once again Mum had to save as much money as she could but also ended up getting a credit card, as again she needed to buy presents for Dad and his family. Once we were there, Mum and I began noticing that some things were not quite right. Dad was busy with work, spending little time with us, though appeared to have more time for his family and had closer bonds with my cousins than with me. He was playful, attentive, and supportive towards them, but more critical towards me, including his opinions about my character and the way I dressed.

Even though Dad was not around and did not contribute much towards my upbringing, he was very forthcoming in verbally attacking Mum and I. Looking back, I really feel for Mum for having done so much and supporting me as much as she could, only to be faced with criticism for not raising me right. Dad did not try to make up for not being with us, not only during our time in the US but also for leaving us in the UK.

Not only was Dad hardly ever around, but he also behaved strangely during our time in the US. I remember one morning during breakfast when I asked Mum to get me something from the fridge and as she went to open the fridge door, Dad rushed over and opened the freezer door above, letting a frozen turkey fall and hit the back of Mum's head. Mum had almost lost consciousness and let out an agonising scream. What I found myself being dumbfounded by was not only Dad's lack of response, but also that he did not get anything from the freezer and left to go to work. The loud thud from the frozen turkey hitting mum and her agonising scream really got me to the core.

A few days later, whilst Mum was making the bed one morning, she noticed a small plastic bag containing black powder under her pillow. When she showed it to Dad, he simply shrugged his shoulders and did not say anything about it. There was no one else at the property so it had to be something he knew about. Was Dad trying to harm Mum? The thought was utterly unimaginable.

Days passed and our time in the US and with Dad was not as enjoyable as we thought it would be. I vividly remember a morning when Mum had done some laundry and was putting away Dad's clothes. Just as she was putting Dad's socks away, she noticed a box

THE WAR IN ME

in the same drawer which she opened, and in it was Dad's passport. Dad's reason for not being able to come over to see us was that he had sent his passport off for renewal, so what was his passport doing there?! There was more. As Mum opened the wardrobe, she saw another box which she opened and was filled with photos. No ordinary photos, but photos of Dad standing next to different landmarks with his arms wrapped around young women. There were also photos which were more explicit, again of him with various women. Mum tried to hide them from me, just as she had always tried to hide her sadness and pain, but I was there and could not un-see what I saw. Dad had gone to work and even if he had been around, I'm not sure whether he would have acknowledged Mum's distress. He probably wouldn't have had anything to say about what she discovered and most likely have accused her of snooping around. At the same time, no explanation could have excused what was seen in those photos. What was also distressing for both Mum and I to see were the clothes he was wearing in the photos. They were clothes she had picked for Dad when he visited us as well as those she had bought for him.

In the same box, under the collection of photos, were cassettes with recordings of Mum's conversations with different people. Mum had no idea that she was being recorded, and it was a terrible thing for Dad to have done. He had always seen Mum as a sincere and honest person, and it was these traits which had drawn Dad towards her, so why did he do such a thing? My theory is that Dad, having been as deceitful as he was, could not contemplate how Mum would remain loyal. What must have been even more bizarre for Dad to hear from the recordings was Mum speaking to friends and family about how she was excited for us to be able to spend time with him.

Following such discoveries, Mum began packing our belongings and called my cousin who lived nearby to come and pick us up. As we were about to leave, Mum saw Dad's youngest sister and wanted to inform her of our reason for leaving. This sister was probably the one who caused the most tension in Mum and Dad's relationship, even in the early days before they got married, and she tried to dissuade Dad from marrying Mum. Even after they were married, this aunt was interfering and would say very harsh things to Mum, simply because Mum's family background was different to theirs, being the fuel for a majority of Mum and Dad's arguments. Mum went over to my aunt to say she could not tolerate Dad's actions and had decided to leave. My aunt's response could not have been any more disrespectful or unkind, and not much different to how she had always been towards Mum. Her response was that Mum should have known it was inevitable that Dad would act in such ways and was the price she would pay for marrying a man with wealth.

For some reason, certain members of Dad's family could not understand that Mum had no hidden agenda for marrying Dad; it was purely because she had fallen in love with a man who showed himself to be a kind, caring and loving person and who expressed commitment to being with her. It is probably because those family members really knew Dad and that one day his true being would be exposed. Mum was utterly taken aback by my aunt's comment and felt completely attacked and defenceless. I could sense shock, hurt, anguish, and anger building up inside of Mum as my aunt was following us to the door to get us out of the house as quickly as possible. At this point, Mum could no longer contain her feelings and screamed, 'You murderer! You killed my children. I will never forgive you!'

This very aunt had forcefully given Mum a concoction of things to terminate her first pregnancy, which led to complications around Mum's subsequent pregnancies. It was because of this that Mum needed to be bed-bound for the later stages of a pregnancy to increase the chances of survival. Having to give birth to multiple dead babies had led to Mum feeling dead inside, and in this moment, there was a lot she was feeling inside of her. For the first time, Mum confronted this aunt, and it must have been some relief for her after having carried such pain for all those years.

Mum opened the door and standing outside was my cousin who appeared very concerned for us. As we started bringing our luggage outside and were about to leave, I got a sense that we were being watched. As I glanced at a window on the upper floor of the house, I saw this aunt standing there with her middle finger up. I remember feeling bewildered, disappointed, rejected, and full of rage.

CHAPTER 8

Captive to pain and hurt

I remember Mum being utterly distraught as she began telling my cousin all that had happened since we had been in the US. The next morning, as my cousin opened his front door, he discovered eggshells following an egg attack, and we were pretty sure whose doing it was. Dad's family knew where we were going to stay until our departure back to London. Both Mum and I could not wait to return home to be as far as possible from Dad and his family and distance ourselves from all the hurt we had endured during our time in the US.

Once we arrived at the airport, we were confronted with another very distressing encounter. This time it involved us being taken into an investigation room where all our belongings and we ourselves were physically searched, as airport officials had received information that we were in possession of illegal items.

It was clear that Dad was not going to be happy about finally being caught after years of Mum defending him and their relationship. He would say to her, 'It's all in your head,' whenever Mum did question or express any doubt about his behaviour. The psychological attacks followed Mum and I even after we returned home where we received endless calls during all hours of the day and night. No

45

matter how much we attempted to escape, the torment felt never-ending and eventually Mum had no choice but to change our phone number.

Revelations continued as Mum and I tried to come to terms with the marital breakdown and create a new life without Dad. One of these revelations was that Dad had shown interest towards a family member and had even attempted making advances towards them. Mum, in her mind, went back to all the times she had been told about Dad being deceitful and it was only now she could believe what she had previously heard. She thought she could believe Dad as he was convincing and reassuring in his words. 'They're jealous of what we have.' 'You're worrying over nothing.' 'You're the only one in my life and I would never betray your trust' were things Dad would say to Mum whenever she brought up some of the things people were saying to her about him. Mum had sacrificed her youth, dreams, and aspirations to be with Dad, who to her was everything. Going from him being everything to now being nothing was a big ask for Mum. She had always shown her commitment towards Dad, even whilst waiting for the day when she believed the three of us would be together. Despite Dad being away for long periods of time, he was never far from Mum's mind. Those closest to Mum advised her not to spend any more of her life waiting hopefully for Dad, as it became apparent how the commitment on his part was not mutual.

Mum really began questioning whether Dad's love for her had ever been real. It definitely felt real on Mum's part. Dad had professed his love for Mum and how she was everything to him. He had expressed to Mum that he would never intentionally do anything to hurt her and yet hurt was exactly what had been done.

Following the breakdown of her relationship with Dad, Mum went to a jeweller to sell her engagement ring and use the money to pay towards my education. She could not believe what she discovered; the ring she had been given by Dad, which all these years she had believed was a real diamond, was in fact not real. I was not with Mum at the time and when I came home, I could sense her feelings of shame for being deceived by Dad in such a way. 'Was anything ever real? Was I ever in the right mind to think that our love for each other was genuine?' cried Mum. What was real was how utterly distraught and unvalued she felt in the relationship.

Mum was once told by an old friend she had bumped into, that Dad had contacted her and accused Mum of having spoken ill of her and her family. Not only that, but Dad had also heavily discouraged the friend from having any contact with Mum. As a matter of fact, Dad had said similar things to various family friends with the intent of reducing Mum's social contacts and support network.

Another old friend informed Mum that Dad had set up multiple businesses and had invested in properties. What is more is that he had at the same time set up another family, another life, all unbeknown to Mum and I. Apparently, I had another half-sister younger than me who I never knew existed. She got to spend time with Dad, time I could have had with him, as well as being provided with a home that Dad had bought for her and her mum.

As time went on, Mum and I continued discovering more things about Dad. Another good friend, whose husband was a businessman, described finding out from his cousin that Dad had sold properties worth huge sums of money. Dad was not only emotionally and psychologically neglectful, but he had also provided very little financially for Mum and I. Just as he could have left us to become "minced meat" if we were still living in Afghanistan, Dad did leave us without considering what we needed to survive and make life more manageable.

I am aware how some people who have experienced neglect or abuse of some kind can find it difficult to speak out or find a way out. For Mum, her way out was really listening to such revelations, which enabled her to break away from the trust and investment she had had in her relationship with Dad. Over time, Mum began to realise she was a person with wisdom, courage, capability, and resilience. She recognised she had the ability to live her own life and was also able to be encouraging of me to do the same.

This was not easy and took time. It involved Mum beginning to recognise and address years of different forms of abuse, emotional suffering, and pain, and what followed was a great deal of self-blame and torment on her part for choosing to make a life with a person like Dad. On some level Mum believed she had failed to emulate the loving relationship she had witnessed between her mother and father. Mum also believed she had failed as a mother as I did not have the father I deserved. It was also a significant loss: loss of time, opportunities, of having the children she miscarried, her health and trust and confidence in herself as well as other people. Moreover, Mum did not have the rights that every person is ultimately entitled to, including the right to freely express herself and the right to pursue an education and career. She was truly deprived of a lot of things I take for granted. However, I believe the biggest loss was for Dad, as he sabotaged being in a loving relationship, and losing a daughter who a lot of people would be extremely proud of. The emotional scars from the ongoing pain Mum endured during her relationship with Dad is something she is trying her best to overcome, even up to this day.

CHAPTER 9

Rejection

The reality is that we all encounter some form of rejection at times in our lives, from society, relationships, as well as ourselves.

Rejection may be reflected in society's inability to embrace, accommodate, and respond to the needs of its citizens, and where there are impediments towards an individual's needs and rights. This is something I encountered when the war in Afghanistan broke out.

Regarding relationships, it may be compelling for an individual to fulfil the expectations of others in order to feel valued. However, this is likely to create difficulty in the person getting to know and be in touch with who they are. A person may believe they have invested a great deal and given all they can in the process but may end up feeling that not all of them is being acknowledged and responded to.

Rejection has played a significant role during different parts of my life which I believe began early on and even before I was born. From what I know, Dad was not particularly happy when Mum shared the news of her pregnancy and told her to abort it, to get rid of me. When I was a baby there was an occasion when my half-sister found her way into my bedroom where I was sleeping and wanted to tamper with my milk with the intent of poisoning me.

Coming to the UK, I experienced further rejection, first by Dad disregarding what Mum and I needed to survive in an unfamiliar place, leaving us to fend for ourselves. There have been various occasions where Mum and I have encountered rejection including regarding our race and ethnicity. I distinctly recall a neighbour shouting, 'Why are you here? Go back to your country!' Feeling as though I do not belong has also led to me rejecting and in some ways dismissing parts of me. Adding rejection to the mix of not feeling good enough, clever enough, worthy enough, capable enough, strong enough, left me disconnected from myself, finding it difficult to acknowledge feelings and emotions which were being stirred in me. I have also witnessed Mum encounter different forms of rejection to the point of being rejecting of herself and her existence.

I have at times encountered rejection from others whereby my values, aspirations, and commitments have been undermined. Some people have gone so far as imposing their own values on me, making out that they are living life the "right way", which led to some relationships breaking down.

Regarding Dad, both Mum and I were hopeful that in time he would see the distress he had caused and to attempt to make contact to put things right, or at least apologise for what he had put us through. Days, weeks, months passed where we heard nothing from him, and even though Mum was resolute in not having any contact with Dad, she still carried hope that he would attempt to restore his relationship me, and she gave us every opportunity possible to make things work.

I remember being in two minds about re-establishing contact, having carried the pain of what I had witnessed. As more time went by, Mum heard through a friend that Dad had undergone a heart operation. In contrast to Dad's un-emphatic response towards Mum and her health, she was quick to see this as a reason for me to initiate contact with Dad. She encouraged me to send Dad a get-well card, and a few days after I called him to ask how he was doing.

To my disappointment, and despite his health issues, he was still the same person, in the sense that he carried on from where he left off, verbally attacking and putting blame on Mum. He had completely rejected the fact that he was responsible for the break-down of his relationship with Mum, as well as our relationship. No matter how much I tried, it was as if I was on a battlefield, under attack by Dad's cruel words being fired at me. I did not have such weapons at my disposal, and my only source of self-protection was to disengage and to completely reject the thought that there was potential for Dad and I to have a relationship. I could not accept what Dad was saying as well as not saying, and it was time for me to reject him and his opinions once and for all. Even though I was sure in myself that I had rejected our relationship, I still found it difficult to detach from all the horrible things he had said to Mum and I, as well as the ways he had behaved and let us down.

Recounting the last time we visited Dad in the US, Mum had found that Dad had put the photos she had sent of me into a shoe box at the bottom of his cupboard. Metaphorically speaking, Dad had boxed me up and had pushed me to one side, and I needed to do the same towards him. What I found the hardest was wanting to reject the biological connection between him and I. I can see some of the physical resemblance I have to him and have strived hard to reject there being any other affiliation.

There have been times when I have wondered whether it would have been better if I was never born, though I imagine life would have been very different for Mum. She may have come to believe that her wanting to become a mother was constantly being rejected and contrary to Dad, Mum has been anything but rejecting towards me.

I believe rejection can at times be necessary and can lead to more optimal ways of being and relating. It can enable us to exercise choice in what we accept and tolerate, what really matters to us and what we need to disregard.

I have for example, rejected the belief that I am incapable and unworthy. Whenever I am faced with rejection it serves as a reminder for me to be committed and invested in being kind and accepting towards myself. For instance, encountering negative judgement from certain people around my academic capabilities, I genuinely believed there was no way I could pursue education to university level. At the same time, I also recognised the value I place on education and remember telling myself that I could learn in a way that I found constructive and fulfilling. I was truly inspired by Mum's side of the family who had their own challenges, yet they did not reject the importance of achieving their academic potential. I knew that

I needed to develop my knowledge and skills in a way which I believed would be achieved by studying at degree level. I saw university as being a place which would offer me teaching, guidance, tools, and resources and help me develop my confidence, which at times had been trampled on. Dad having rejected Mum's desire to go to university made her do the complete opposite when it came to me. She supported and encouraged me to study what I wanted and the way I wanted to. Mum's support and encouragement as well as my determination, commitment, and investment led me to undertake and complete a degree before going on to do two master's degrees. The learning gained from university, as well as from work experience and the lessons life taught me, enabled me to go into a career I am truly passionate about. I am deeply grateful to Mum for not giving up on me, and I am pleased I didn't give up on myself either.

I have come to the realisation that I no longer want to reject what I need and value. In many ways writing this book has enabled me to acknowledge what I have needed as well as what I give value to. It has allowed me to reflect on how driven I have become, having turned into reality some of the things which were once a dream.

CHAPTER 10

I feel your pain

Having always had a close relationship Mum, I have at times joked with her about how I started being there for her from when she was pregnant with me and have been there ever since. I believe there is truth in that, as it was a time when Mum was completely alone, far from home and loved ones; yet she had me, and I literally could not be any closer to her.

Mum has spoken about how throughout her pregnancy, even though she was reassured by medical professionals that everything would be OK, she carried a great deal of anxiety and worry about something happening to me whilst at the same time feeling comforted by me being with her. Mum had always been good at talking with me about different issues, which she navigated according to my age and emotional capacity.

I can imagine it being a real dilemma for Mum; on the one hand, I was the closest person to her, especially once we had separated from family and friends, and on the other hand, she needed to hold certain things back from me. I would say that Mum was in fact still communicating with me, although at a subconscious level and beyond her awareness. There were many times that Mum fretted over how she could make life better for us, and was confronted with different battles involving health, relationships, losses, and countless setbacks.

As I have grown older, I have striven to not only support Mum but also protect her from further adversity and would say that Mum and I have shared many anxieties. The first couple of months after I was born, Mum continued feeling extremely anxious around my survival to the point that she kept a mirror under my pillow and would use it to check my breathing. Growing up, I developed extreme anxiety around Mum's survival, and found myself regularly checking her breathing, quick to feel unease around the condition of her health.

At the same time, I have learnt a substantial amount about resilience from Mum, which has led to me taking on and managing some of Mum's issues. If Mum is OK, then I can feel more assured and OK in myself. I know it is not completely possible to protect a person from all kinds of difficulty, and I see it more as wishful thinking on my part. I have strived to be there for Mum in whatever way I can in resolving and lessening the impact different events and encounters may pose.

In some ways, I believe I am representing various people in Mum's life who have not been there. I have found myself taking on things for Mum, sometimes without consulting her which has created tension in our relationship, where she has viewed herself as incapable, or even a burden.

Following on from the previous chapter, I have come to view rejection as an injection of psychological and emotional pain. The rejection I have encountered from certain relationships and situations has made me realise that the pain can be a gift in disguise. I would go as far in saying that the biggest rejection, that which I experienced from Dad, was ironically the biggest gift.

I am certain that many readers have experienced different types of emotional pain and it may be rather difficult to perceive such an experience as a gift. For me, the pain enabled me to develop insight and a deep empathy. It has led to me being able to form strong emotional connections with others, both at a personal and professional level. I find myself attuned to what another person is "at war" with, and am understanding, respectful, and appreciative of how individuals navigate emotional conflict.

For example, I understand how a person may try to block out pain and how that can create difficulties. For some, it may mean that the pain they find themselves in has rendered them helpless and unable to see a way out. There are also individuals who may want to confront their pain head on, and the way it is confronted is inevitably going to be different from one person to the next. Not only that, but what else a person has going on and what else they believe they need in their lives can impact the way they approach their distress.

I would say my approach has been somewhat varied in the sense that there have been occasions when I have tried my hardest to be disregarding, wanting to avoid, not being acknowledging of what I need to best help myself. At other times, I have felt like there is nothing I can do to change what I perceive as permanent and unfixable, which has created anger and resentment. I have felt fearful and apprehensive about the overwhelming state I may find myself in if I was to look pain in the eye. Can I provide myself with protection and safety from what may feel like an emotional minefield? For some time, I believed that if I were to confront my pain, it would mean accepting that I had been hurt and that other people and events had exerted control over my life. I have struggled with the prospect of making myself feel vulnerable again, yet understood that by confronting the pain, I would be exercising control over it. Furthermore, confronting pain has also enabled me to confront some of the judgement I have held towards myself, appreciating that life is not easy. In all such responses, I have come to realise that pain never completely disappears, and it can be triggered at times we do not anticipate. If a person can allow themself to confront their pain in their own way, it can lessen its impact. I also believe it can be helpful to remind ourselves of the pain we have gone through because it is part of our experience and the reality of living an authentic life.

Early in my life, although it was a bumpy journey, I enjoyed what I saw, explored, and experienced. As I continued life's journey, I had to navigate different routes. There have been some one way and closed off roads, symbolic of the difficulties around some relation-ships and encounters. There have also been some very long winding roads, where no matter how much I strived to make something happen, the road appeared never-ending. Metaphorically speaking, I have also travelled along roads where I have come across a junction: time to slow down, pause, assess, and reflect. In some instances what has followed has been a roundabout of different options, and thus possibilities and opportunities.

I believe we all have very different journeys with previous experiences forming the roadmap which we are guided by. I also believe we have a choice as to whether we want to use our past as a guide or if there is another way of mapping things out. Moreover, we may want to use a different means of getting from one place to another. I have, at times, wanted to get out of the car and go on foot to explore the environment up close. At other times I have thought of getting into a helicopter to have a broader view of places I have been to and come from, as well as the many more which are on the horizon.

I would say that I have survived, and to survive has involved offering myself the opportunity to experience situations which are emotionally compelling. If I had not survived some of the adversity that life can expose us to, I would not have been able to write about them in this book. I would not have been able to tell myself that I am able to push through and overcome difficulties and do so in ways I did not imagine. For some time, I found myself experiencing the dissonance of not wanting to have gone through hurtful events, and recognising the wisdom, strength, courage, as well as hope that such events have created. It would have been rather nice to have been able to live in a country where war did not cause us to flee, and to have been close to extended family. A life which offered abundance in many respects. But then again, it was possible that we would be confronted with different situations, and it is hard to say what options and possibilities we would have had. Moving homes and exposing myself to new environments meant sometimes I felt rejected and led me to disconnect, but others created essential opportunities in getting me to the places I wanted to get to and connect with.

I sometimes wonder what it would have been like if Mum's pregnancies had been successful, and I had siblings as well as a loving Dad. However, I feel I have had a family, even though it has only comprised of Mum. This has made me realise the value of investing in my relationship with her and taught me about the significance of having a supportive relationship. Mum's offer of a wealth of love, support, guidance, and encouragement is something I have been able to invest in my relationship with myself. Over the years creating more space to connect with my feelings and emotions, including the more painful ones, has allowed me to ensure I connect with others in their pain, leading me to truthfully say, 'I feel your pain.'

CHAPTER 11

A war of many

Khala Shahgul's tragic death from a bomb explosion in Kabul still hits me hard. We learned that even though Mum and I had left Afghanistan, in my auntie's final moments she was calling for me to save her life as she believed I had become a doctor. To this day, Mum also holds a great deal of guilt over not being able to get members of her family out of Afghanistan.

I feel extremely angry with my motherland for letting its citizens down in not providing safety. I feel angered by others invading and taking over a place which was once only entered by foreign nationals as a holiday destination. During such a time Mum worked in a travel agency arranging tours for holiday makers; that was until she met Dad.

Mum spoke with me about having a close relationship with her dad, which unfortunately was short lived due to his passing when Mum was just eleven years old. To this day Mum speaks of her dad with fondness and admiration, keeping hold of loving memories she has of him and their time together. Mum still feels her dad has a strong presence in her life, who she seeks emotional support, guidance, and protection from. I am aware that Mum also wanted the relationship between Dad and I to have been the same, which I did too.

Growing up I remember eagerly waiting for Dad to return home to Mum and I. That sense of hope entered my recurring dreams, where Dad is with us, something that I have I mentally battled with over the years. Why was I having such dreams particularly after our relationship had broken down? I somehow found it hard to believe he had abandoned Mum and I. I have tried to get to grips with what made Dad do the things he did and did not do as well as his lack of commitment towards us.

What had become another mental battle for me was how little money Dad had been giving us whilst I was a child. We were being given this money through a family friend who believed Dad would pay back, so it was the friend's money, not Dad's. It transpired that Dad had no intention of paying back this friend and instead put it on me to do so once I had reached adulthood. In other words, it was another thing Dad did not provide us with and instead we were left to fend for ourselves.

When I think about whether I was able to get anything from Dad, what I would say is that I got plenty from what he did not give me; I got determination, passion, dedication, freedom, and choice. Mum sees some of the traits, values, and beliefs she has as being passed on from her dad. These are things which Mum has passed on to me, and so I have received valuable gifts from a dad, from my granddad.

Mum and I being forced to abandon what we had in Afghanistan, being pushed out of what was ours and having our livelihoods taken away has created difficulty in understanding where we belong and if we belong anywhere. The ongoing wars in different parts of the world takes me back to how Mum and I struggled for survival, which is something we have continued to do as we have been met with different threats and forms of attack. Disclosing my country of origin is something I do with care and only if necessary, as a way of protecting myself as well as Afghanistan. It is my way of conveying that there is more to me than simply where I am from, and there is more to Afghanistan than what has been depicted in the media. I do not want to be tarnished in the same way as the wars have created damage to Afghanistan's formation and reputation. Undoubtedly, life events and encounters have taken a toll on me, and it can be said that I have survived many wars. Both Mum and I, as well as Afghanistan, have been through a great deal, though it is not the end of any of us. In spite of not having choice when leaving my country of origin, I have kept with me the unique, fond, and vivid memories of my time there. Remembering how Afghanistan was at the time is something I feel I can exercise control over.

Over the years I have noticed how even whilst sleeping I am trying to survive something, as I tend to have very vivid and anxiety provoking dreams, some of which re-occur as if to tell me that there is something I need to revisit. I experience my dreams as very real and pervasive and often feel as though I can never escape from the pain that has been so difficult to put to rest.

I have come to know how people can be at war with themselves, in their relationships, with social, economic, and political environments, and it is about understanding how such battles can be resolved.

A therapist I used to see told me how my feelings of anger were akin to me holding a hot coal in my hand, that it was something I was hurting myself with, which I found difficult to relate to. Over the years I have seen my anger and the hurt that is part of it as reflecting the deep sorrow, anguish and rage that stirs in me as I bear witness to injustices, with the war of many becoming the war in me.

CHAPTER 12

The war in me

Have you ever heard of the saying, "Tired of feeling tired?" It is something I have been grappling with for many years. It was inevitable that the some of the mental and emotional pain I encountered was going to leave its imprint in me, quite literally.

The first and most vivid recollection I have of the physical manifestation of my psychological distress was strangely enough, during a holiday in Dubai. I can imagine some readers may be wondering how is it possible to be in pain when you are on holiday and away from various stressors? Up until then I was relatively confident when it came to my health and do not recall acquiring any major injuries or illnesses. What became clear as the years went by was that I had sustained psychological injuries which had emotional as well as physical implications. Going back to our time in Dubai, it had become a regular holiday destination after Mum and I became fascinated by it from the very first time we visited, and we ended up returning there every year after that. Dubai was truly mesmerising and every time we went back, we noticed the developments which had taken place, and during each of our visits, I made sure we were having a memorable stay.

Every time was memorable, yet what was oddly the most memorable was one of the times when Mum and I went shopping. It was quite early in the day, and we had not done anything particularly physically demanding. The shop that we had visited was one we had been to the previous year, and one of the shop assistants commented that he had noticed I was tired this time and the time before as I had asked for a chair to sit on. I was taken aback by the comment and remember feeling quite embarrassed and annoyed. Some time passed before I began to take notice of more and more instances when I was hit with extreme tiredness, aches and pains, stiffness, piercing, stabbing, and burning sensations. I became aware of experiencing difficulties with concentration, sleep, and mood. I was also experiencing strong palpitations, jitteriness, and a deep pain and beating sensation in my gut and over time, the combination of the mental, emotional, and physical states I found myself in created frustration as well as concern.

I ended up seeking medical advice and after undergoing several tests and examinations, there were no apparent medical concerns. I still found it concerning however, especially in the way it was impacting me. 'What could it be?' was something I was constantly asking myself and medical professionals. Then I received the answer: 'You have fibromyalgia' stated my GP. I felt relieved that what I was experiencing was real and recognised, though did not know much about the condition and its treatment. There is relatively little in the form of treatment available for fibromyalgia, and I have had to figure out what I can do to help in managing it. Due to the condition most likely being set off by acute stress, I am sure it is related to the different stressors that I had encountered as well as those I witnessed Mum being confronted with. I believe adverse life events created susceptibility, which heightened my sensitivity towards perceived and subsequent stressors. With the heightened sensitivity came extra vigilance, where I felt I had to be constantly on alert towards potential threats, akin to being on a mental battlefield. Being on such a battlefield does, at times, leave me utterly exhausted and creates a sense of frustration and despair.

Although I can understand that emotional pain can never completely go away, I never thought that I would be plagued by such endless, pain, fatigue, restlessness, feeling captive in my body and mind. I have regularly said to myself, 'How can I make it through the day?!' Why has my psychological and emotional pain got to me so deeply and pervasively?

Writing about my experience of living with fibromyalgia, I compared it to a pandemic such as Covid-19 which caused havoc and distress. For me, I see fibromyalgia as an "indemic", in that it is inside of me and only I know how it feels. On the outside I can appear fine and well, and at times it has been extremely difficult understanding exactly what had been happening. As my own expert, I came to realise that there are various ways and means by which I can support myself in managing fibromyalgia. I alone truly know what I need, and how to best look after myself.

Since being diagnosed with fibromyalgia, I have gradually become more open with myself and others about living with the condition and the impact it can have. I chose the title of this chapter, "The war in me" when describing living with fibromyalgia because living with the condition has undoubtedly felt like a war, where I have felt weapon-less and ill-equipped. One of the battles has been the intense anger and frustration I have towards the different physical, mental, and emotional symptoms. There have been countless times when I have doubted the reality of my symptoms, instead viewing myself as weak and incapable, which in many ways echoed the criticism of certain others in my past; but no, what I am feeling is real. At times I have also wanted to deny that I have such a condition because it forces me to accept that I have been impacted by events and encounters. It has been difficult navigating the feelings I hold towards fibromyalgia, and paradoxically, I have come to appreciate it. Fibromyalgia has given me the ability to really feel and sense what I am experiencing and has developed my capacity to reflect on and process how I am impacted by what it is I am relating to.

I can also appreciate how others may feel like they are at war with themselves for having to live with a health condition; at war with others for not being understanding or supportive, and at war with medical professionals or healthcare system regarding treatment.

As living beings, I believe we are porous and permeable to different life events and situations which shape the person we become. There are experiences which we find energizing and enriching, and others we may find overwhelming and consuming. Some encounters can be a one-off whereas others may happen more regularly or even be a constant in our lives. When it comes to vulnerability, what can arise is the need for protection, and I have felt a constant need to protect Mum and I from adversities. At the same time, I try to allow my body and mind to understand that there is no real, or at least no imminent threat, where I find myself saying, 'You're fine, I'm fine. You're OK, I'm OK.'

Following on from the previous chapter, it is through my body that I can sense another person's distress, to really feel for and with them. As time has gone by, I have begun to view living with fibromyalgia as an invaluable gift despite it being an outcome of different vulnerabilities and stressors. It has broadened my sense of curiosity, understanding, courage, and strength. Just like I feel a great deal of pain, discomfort, and associated sensations, I am also able to deeply feel more positive emotions and internal states, being able to embody, embrace, and immerse myself in them. Despite fibromyalgia having created tremendous stress and anxiety in me, I know there is more in me and of me which is triumphant.

CHAPTER 13

Worrier and warrior

'Don't worry.'

'Stop worrying.'

'You're such a worrier.'

The above may be things you have said to yourself, have said to others or others have said about you.

Many of us may be under the impression that there is a way of "fixing" ourselves, which can create much anguish.

'You're unfixable.'

'You're not capable of getting anything right.'

'You've failed yourself and a mother who has done everything she could possibly do for you.'

'Worry is endless, it cannot be overcome.'

These are some of the thoughts I have had when I have found myself worrying, fretting, and feeling anxious about all kinds of events and situations. For example, I worry about how much pain and tiredness I am going to experience in a day, I worry about Mum and her health, I worry about getting things wrong, or getting blamed or accused of something which I anticipate having dire consequences.

Some of my worries are ongoing and some are about future and anticipated situations. Worry for me has created a preoccupation, a sense of dread and at times, panic.

What was fuelling some of my worries was the belief that I should not let it get to me which caused pressure and stress to accumulate. 'I am capable and can do and be,' was what I tried to say to myself. Moving forward, my intention was to acknowledge the worry and how I am connecting with it in order to be able to source what is needed. Part of this was acknowledging that worry is OK and normal, and actually necessary in that it can be functional and constructive. Worry can be an umbrella term for a myriad of emotions, thoughts, processes, and actions, which we can navigate and engage with in such a way where we do not feel taken off guard or defeated by.

There have been countless times when I have found myself on high alert to my worried state, feeling the need to be on guard and prepared to take action. My continuous efforts to be and act in such a way has brought up feelings which I have been overwhelmed and even consumed by. I became aware of how more often than not I took on a defenceless position and found myself even less prepared to respond. It was worry itself, which was causing havoc and creating a barrier, getting in the way of living a more engaging and fulfilling life. I needed to find another way to acknowledge my worries and engage more constructively with them.

The chronic worry I was exposing myself to and the associated stress led to my vision becoming compromised. It can be said that the stress of worrying made me see things differently. It was a pivotal moment for me, which led me to re-assess my relationship with worry and the meaning and purpose it had in my life. I realised how for me, worry is purposeful and necessary, albeit in different ways and degrees. Through writing this book, I have come to give a new perspective to worry and have created the below acronym for it:

W – Well-intended
O – Optimal,
R – Reasonable and Responsive acts
R – Relating to
Y – You.

You may have heard of the saying, "Beauty is in the eye of the beholder", which has led me to develop an appreciation of worry. I can see how through the shift in perspective, I have gone from being passive, controlled and overwhelmed by worry, to now seeing it as a resource and aid. In certain ways worry has parallels with the way I try to offer myself different routes and modes of getting to different places. I can for example identify how worrying about pain enables me to consider and work out ways of managing it. For certain other worries I realise it may be in my best interest to create steps towards a more favourable outcome. When it came to what I was going to do as a career, I can truly say I gave myself a number of options. For me, it was important to do a job which I had a deep personal investment in and which I could make a significant contribution to.

I remember not being completely certain of the exact work I would go on to do, yet I knew it was going to be in mental health, and for that I felt it was necessary for me to go to university. I knew that I needed to prepare financially and that it was going to require a great deal of commitment on my part. Throughout my time in college and at university, I held down different jobs and even when it came to the jobs I did, I wanted to ensure they were going to be engaging as well as giving me different opportunities to develop my confidence and social interaction skills.

Becoming aware of the energy that worry can take up, I wanted to ensure I worried in the "right way." That may sound a bit strange, yet it is something which has been particularly helpful for me, and this is where visualisation has been a great resource. Every day, where possible, I give myself the opportunity to assess how I am feeling. I may notice physically feeling tense, restless, heavy, suffocated, or even numb. Emotionally I may be experiencing feelings of fear, unease, and dread. Mentally, my thinking, concentration, and motivation may be fluctuating, or creating a barrier, especially if I am, either consciously or subconsciously, wanting to avoid the worry. I begin to visualise myself walking into an imaginary walk-in wardrobe and as I do, telling myself that I am choosing to respond to my worried state. I believe this way of relating to my internal and external worlds enables myself to be more acknowledging of them and to choose to interact more engagingly with them. Once I am in the wardrobe, I give myself opportunity to look around and pick out a worry, or a few worries depending on the size, role, and impact of the worry, as well as the amount of physical, mental, and emotional energy I need to have for them and the day. I would describe it similarly to picking out an outfit where you may say 'Right, today I am going to wear this with that.'

Once I am in the imaginary wardrobe, I say to myself something along the lines of 'Today, although I am feeling tired, I do find myself having sufficient energy to focus on a biggish and a smaller worry,' looking around for those size worries. On certain days I may choose to focus my energy and attention on similar worries which I am more likely to find near one another. Metaphorically speaking, I can pick out a top which may be a certain colour, fabric, and density, representing the nature, feel, and weight of a worry. If it is a prominent worry, I may choose a deep colour with a heavier fabric. If the worry is less prominent, I may choose a lighter colour and texture to reflect it, and I tend to do the same regarding the bottom half of my worry outfit. In this walk-in wardrobe I also imagine there being accessories which are worries I have previously resolved. I can put on these accessories as a way of offering myself encouragement, support, strength, and grounding.

With visualisation comes a new vision, another possibility and reality. Staying with the imaginary wardrobe, once the day is over, I can decide where I am going to put what I wore. I may for instance want to put the worry or worries back in the same place if I feel more time and opportunity is needed to work with it or them. I may want to put a worry in another place, for example, folding and putting it in a drawer if it does not need to be that visible, and can pick it up at a later time. There may be worries which I have been able to resolve over the course of the day, and I may decide to get rid of them because they are no longer necessary to keep.

Just how clothes can be worn to make a statement, be a way of expressing ourselves, function like armour or be a form of protection, they can also make us feel more prepared and confident to take on what we have going on. That is why for me, viewing worries as different pieces of clothing has not only created a different perspective and offered me another way of approaching them, but it also captures the reality that I tend to embody my feelings and emotions. I can and have since been able to more consciously and purposely decide what worry to put on myself and address in the way I "dress" for the day.

CHAPTER 14

Loss

Avoid! Avoid! Avoid! That's exactly what I wanted to do when it came to approaching this topic. I cannot imagine loss being easy for anyone to deal with, and over the years I have tried to create steps and strategies in approaching this area. The reality is that we can never be completely ready to approach loss. Loss means someone or something being taken away from us, which I would say Mum and I have experienced in abundance.

Loss for us began with the loss of a beautiful country which I had no choice but to leave due to the impending war and lack of safety. Associated with the loss was the loss of family, friends, and other significant people and relationships. Subsequent losses followed which I have and will continue referring to.

Having provided emotional support to countless individuals including whilst working as a bereavement helpline volunteer, I recognised how the loss of a loved one can make other things present for a bereaved individual, such as there being a sense of emptiness, meaningless, void, and bleakness. Being bereaved left some questioning the meaning of life and feeling as though they had lost part of themselves, not knowing who they truly were or could be without the person in their lives.

When I think about life, I think of it as being on a trajectory; after we are born, we go through and encounter a series of changes as part of our development, where loss is almost inevitable. The losses associated with the natural course of human development can lead to gains where we are becoming more of ourselves and fulfilling our potential. Despite it being something we have little control over, the way we approach transitions is imperative and impacted by how embrace what life can offer us. In life we undoubtedly experience all kinds of change; there are those which we may actively contribute to where we can see how they can be promotive, and others which have come about from adversity. The latter types are likely to have detrimental, devastating, and long-lasting effects, such as that of Covid-19, resulting in various losses. For example, the government's response to Covid-19 created a loss of freedom during lockdowns, along with isolation, disconnection, deprivation, and for many, created a sense of defeat. The losses also included the loss of trust and faith towards people in authority and those making significant decisions. With the loss of control associated with a pandemic like Covid-19, what has arisen for many individuals has been a determination to exercise control in other ways and areas of their lives.

I recall initially being in disbelief upon hearing about the virus and the potential ramifications it was likely to pose. At the time I was working in a college as a counsellor and wellbeing advisor. I was in a session with a student who expressed extreme fear about there being a virus in circulation and felt very angered by the lack of concern he saw in others. Looking back, I actually think I was one of those people showing a lack of concern as I tried to help the student challenge his thinking and perception. It was not long after that the pandemic hit, and we were at war with a deadly virus. It was devasting seeing and hearing about lives being lost, people losing loved ones as well as the lives they had made for themselves. Mum and I were also challenged by the possibility of our lives being hit hard from the pandemic and was yet another "war" we needed to battle with.

Due to Mum's complex health, she fell into the category termed "extremely clinically vulnerable." I remember how during the first lockdown we did not leave the house for almost a month due to the immense fear we carried. It was another point in time when I needed to protect Mum and I from threat.

Over the course of the pandemic, I learnt more about the importance of prioritisation and the things that mattered the most such as our health and wellbeing, being authentic, practising gratitude, kindness, generosity, and increasing my faith in humanity. I spent most of the pandemic working from home, which initially came about due to me expressing concern if I was to catch the virus and pass it to Mum at a time when no vaccines were available. I was also aware that not everyone had the support they needed. The unpredictable, unsafe, and damaging effects of Covid-19 were in some ways mirrored in the actions of citizens. Many people found it difficult to know how to react or respond, feeling stuck, perplexed, angered, and frustrated.

In many respects the risks associated with the virus encouraged a devil-may-care attitude for some individuals who took other risks, stepping into the unknown, whilst for others it involved standing their ground, finding voice and expression. The havoc created by the pandemic focused attention on how society needs to look after and support its people. Covid-19 in many ways contributed to other responses from individuals, including viewing the pandemic as offering an opportunity to try to do things differently or even try something completely new.

What I do know is that different losses have led to me wanting to connect with myself and my feelings which were becoming alive. I believe just as loss is a complex phenomenon, the way we face it can also be complex. Loss can with it bring about other types of uncertainty, such as how we are to respond to it.

Sometimes for example it can be very difficult to understand what we can have and want from life. Furthermore, a loss can be akin to a force robbing us of our desires, dreams, and ambitions. I know that for me, there have been moments following an encounter with loss where I questioned and doubted whether I had the capability to move past, navigate around, or continue to live alongside it. I know that for Mum, the losses she felt captive to led her to experience extreme periods of isolation, even to the point of losing who she was.

At times, a loss can seem as if life has turned its back on a person and can be experienced as a point of no return, or possibly lead to subsequent losses. It can result in an individual losing their bearings and they may not feel like they know who they really are, what they need or want. This can in turn create difficulty in knowing where to turn for support. I also believe that loss can offer a different perspective on life and for some can act as a turning point. In addition, setbacks, even those perceived as rejection or abandonment, can lead to a person becoming resolute in running life in a way that suits their own needs.

We may at times question life, which is something I have grappled with from time to time and have also witnessed others doing. What helped me deal with the anguish and the many questions I had was developing a deeper connection with my faith and spirituality. I have begun to see how I am here to experience learning, understanding, and fulfilment. I have not mentioned faith with the intention of encouraging readers to be drawn towards any particular faith, yet to have faith in themselves that they are capable in their own unique way and deserve to live a life which is fulfilling and true to them.

Can loss ever be a good thing? I imagine many readers responding with contempt or confusion as to how that could ever be a possibility. Having reflected on the many losses Mum and I have had, not having Dad in our lives was definitely a good thing. Despite facing a great deal of losses in the process, not having such a person in our lives has made so much more possible; in other words, there has been much gained from the loss.

Mum and I have often imagined how our lives may have panned out if Dad continued to be present. Mum truly believes she would not be here as Dad would most likely have continued being a damaging force. It would have also been very likely that Dad would have attempted to limit what I did with my life. I for instance, could not have foreseen myself studying to the degree I have done or being able to engage in the various pursuits which have been possible as a result. It can be a source of comfort when someone says, 'I'm sorry for your loss.' In the case of Dad however, what I say to Mum and myself is, 'Thank God for such a loss.'

CHAPTER 15

Dreams can come true

I always strive to be grateful for what I have, what has been possible as well as what else may be possible. You may have come across expressions such as "Dream big!" and "Live your wildest dreams!" which seem to suggest that we should want things in abundance or something which may seem unimaginable, uncontainable, or untameable. Dreams from such a perspective can become something we may become so engrossed in that can make our decisions and actions appear callous. Furthermore, if we are given the impression that dreaming is something we should do, the very act of doing so has potential to create pressure, becoming more of a burden than something fulfilling, enriching, or freeing. I believe dreams reflect hope, trust, value, and belief in ourselves, enabling us to reach our full potential, making us more driven and life more meaningful and fulfilling. I am someone who dreams and continues dreaming and where one dream has led to subsequent ones, coming to realise what it is I am feeling inspired about and wanting to embark upon.

It is possible that some of us associate dreams with childhood where we are likely to engage in imaginary pursuits analogous to the aspirations that we may have had. For example, 'When I grow up, I want to be…' For some people dreams provide distraction and help them disconnect from the present, and at times, dire reality of life. Through dreams a person can take themself to a more captivating and enriching space, providing a means of stepping to one side when life becomes overwhelming or consuming. I also see the process of dreaming as enabling an individual to connect with their true calling, which may also involve them stepping out of their comfort zone and taking risks, turning their dreams into reality.

I can see how we may want our lives and the world to be different to the way it currently is. A dream can therefore be akin to having a different vision for the world and the environment we live in. We may want to share such dreams with others, turning it into a bigger dream, one which unites and gets the support it needs. These may be dreams which are intended to have a fundamental collective and societal impact, where people come together for a cause and purpose. Undoubtedly the world is coloured and impacted by different people and their dreams, and it is also important to acknowledge individuals who have dreams but are not so forthcoming or expressive about them. It may be that they feel unworthy or incapable of having what their heart desires. It could also be that some people find themselves assuming responsibility for supporting others in fulfilling their dreams. Furthermore, some individuals may ignite their desires and aspirations in other people and may live their dreams through them. There are also people who may only speak about their dreams if they believe they have been able to make them happen.

Conversely, dreams may have been taken away from a person due to a lack of opportunity, belief, investment, encouragement, or support.

Mum's dream of going to university and establishing herself professionally were dreams taken away from her. When it comes to dreaming, Mum has often had vivid dreams where she has found herself trying to escape and flee different conflicts and turmoil. Even when awake, she has at times felt consumed and trapped by her dreams. For example, for a long time Mum felt stuck by her dream of wanting to become a mother. Every time she encountered the loss of a baby, loved ones would tell her not to put her life and health at stake and to give up on the dream. Mum also became captive to her dream of having a loving partner and for me to have a caring dad, leading to disappointment, guilt, self-blame, and disillusionment. Mum however never stopped dreaming as her dream of becoming a mother eventually came true. This dream becoming a reality provided Mum with the opportunity to nurture her academic and professional dreams through me, being encouraging, supportive, and investing in my academic pursuits.

I have also encountered countless vivid dreams which have seemed very real and can recount times when I have woken up feeling bewildered, not really knowing or being able to discern what is reality. At times, my dreams have been difficult to let go of, particularly those I have felt entrapped by. I believe such dreams communicate the thoughts and meanings I associate with certain events and encounters. My dreams have in many ways been symbolic of what I have been battling with, as well as what I need to attend to and confront. Waking up from such dreams I have sometimes found myself becoming consumed and at the same time feeling surprised by surviving them, noticing the fear and frustration in me attempting to overturn them. I consciously try to re-narrate a story which is being played out in my dreams, to be the author of my own life. At other times I have dreamed of a story line where I am an observer as I cannot determine any personal connection with it. When I wake up however, they drift away, perhaps communicating the things that I have lost connection with. Dreams remind me of my need to be at peace and feel content with what I am stepping into, connecting, and engaging with. Then came the day when I had a different type of dream. Despite it being vivid and seemingly real, I did not feel captive to it and instead found it captivating. In the dream I saw this book and as I have previously mentioned, writing such a book had been a dream of mine. This dream was one I really wanted to hold on to and allow myself to attend to and deeply engage with in my waking life.

The following morning, I remember telling Mum about the dream. As I was recounting it, I became aware of how emotionally invested I had become in the dream and in that sense, in the book. That very day I put pen to paper and began to take the first steps in making that dream a reality.

I intended on using the book to offer Mum and I a medium to communicate our struggles as well as our triumphs and accomplishments.

My dream for the book also involved being coherent with the narrative and my choice of words to highlight the difficulties Mum and I had encountered, as well as the insight, inspiration, and determination which has been ignited by such experiences.

Words for me are a form of expression which I pay close attention to, and which informs how I listen to what I say as well as what I hear from others. I believe we sometimes need to say a lot to express ourselves whilst at other times less is more, where a single word, phrase or statement does all the talking. Words can really capture what a person is feeling and experiencing, and they have the power of dividing as well as uniting people. Through the process of writing, I did experience moments of doubt as to why I was writing about something or the way I was writing about it. I have on many occasions, questioned whether what I am writing is valuable, acceptable, and relatable; is what I am writing about worthy of being recognised and validated? Trying to overcome the fear of potential rejection. I also did not want to overshadow the good moments and memories I could see the value in referring to. It has been through using different words and expressions that I have been able to create meaning and give value to what I have revisited and recounted.

By writing about dreams, I have been able to remind myself of the previous wishes and desires I have had. Despite some not happening, I have still been able to reach many of my dreams. The process enabled me to realise how dreams can be years in the making and just because something does not happen in the way we originally wanted it to; it does not mean it cannot ever happen.

Let me share with you one such dream. As I have previously mentioned, I have been professionally involved in the field of mental health for a substantial period of time. I have taken on various roles and responsibilities with the intention of broadening my understanding and skills. In one of the places I worked, it became clearer to me what it was that I wanted to do, and in order to do this, I needed to go back to university. At that point I had a degree in psychology and a master's in child psychology. I recognised that to go back to studying was a big commitment, though I knew it would get me closer to my dream job. That is not to say that my previous educational pursuits and attainments did not get me anywhere. As a matter of fact, they got me to many places and together with the experience life gave me, I was able to get on a master's programme in counselling and psychotherapy. The training involved me balancing assignments, assessments, placements, personal therapy, two paid jobs, as well as other responsibilities. It also meant that three years of my life was going to be dedicated to this dream. All the while I was engaged in my professional training, I could envisage myself going back to the place I previously worked in though this time working as a psychotherapist.

It undoubtedly required, commitment, determination, investment, and patience on my part. It was five years after me gaining my professional qualification as a counsellor and psychotherapist that I saw a job vacancy in the place I wanted to return to work. Despite having worked in various places and having built up my professional experience, I was unsure whether I was able to offer what the job required. I remember the more I wanted to work there, the more unsure and hesitant I found myself becoming. Tied into this dream was my want to be part of a place where I could professionally establish myself as well as having a professional home where I could experience belonging, connection, and growth. Having since secured this dream job, I can say that even to this day, it feels unreal, almost like a dream, in the way I feel entrusted, valued, and supported in fulfilling my professional potential.

Despite the different commitments, demands, pressures, and challenges, I feel incredibly thankful to Mum and all those who were part of my journey in embarking on and engaging in academia and professional training. From my engagements in the field of mental health and wellbeing, I have been able to listen to and try to understand what makes people do or not do things in their lives, what they have encountered, and the meaning they associate with different experiences. I have gotten to understand people's relationships with society, significant others, as well as themselves, facilitating expression, bearing witness to and being part of an authentic encounter.

I feel extremely fortunate for having this opportunity, partly because I feel in some of my personal relationships it hasn't always been possible to explore, discover, and get to know such things.

Having written about my dreams has not only allowed me to recognise and celebrate past dreams coming true, but it has also led to me acknowledging how dreams have offered me aspiration, hope, commitment, and investment. By dreaming we can make all kinds of things possible and be responsive in the way we acknowledge, connect with, and reach for what we deeply desire.

The following section is a collection of poems which further encapsulates how there can be tensions in our relationship with ourselves, others, and society, and how they can be overcome. The section that follows it offers tools, resources, and practices aimed at promoting mental health and wellbeing.

Seeing ME, seeing YOU, seeing WE through poetry.

What's wrong with me?

There is something wrong with me but what can it be?
I find it so difficult to see.
When I try to stand back and see what is going on,
I question whether there is anything wrong.
For me this is what has always existed,
Which I find hard to create change around,
Though if I do offer myself other ways of being,
The impact can abound.

It's not right!

Why has this happened to me?
Do I deserve it? I must deserve it.
Deep inside of me something does not feel right,
Which is something keeping me up at night.
If only I can shine a light,
To find how this has happened, how it came to be.
It is not a thing I can put my finger on,
Because if I did that, I may be wrong,
But I do know that I need to do something to be able to carry on.

Anxiety

Anxiety can be something that permeates me all over,
Following me around, and moreover,
Making me feel as though I am bound.
Bound to a confined view, narrative, and explanation.
Anxiety can be unfounded,
Though no doubt compounded,
Compounded by the complexities and intricacies of existence,
Which create a sense of persistence.
I am one to persist through insistence,
Trying to navigate the distance,
Between where I am in relativity,
With imagination and reality.
I no longer want to be taken over,
Instead having a hold over,
What I am feeling and being.
And can be sure that it is more than something I am dreaming.

Here I go again

Oh, oh, I did that again,
It's such a pain,
And which I find a drain.
I feel tired from doing the same thing again and again,
It's so damn hard to change my ways from back then.
No, I'm not going to complain,
For it's on me to find another way, other ways,
Because it's not always going to be the same.
Life can feel like such a game,
So I ask myself 'why the shame?'
I need to prioritise what I need,
And that is the right way indeed.

Where did it all go wrong?

I wonder and wonder and think really hard,
Where did it all start?
Was it then… or when…?
It's definitely not easy to say,
And I imagine it always being that way.
It's almost like playing a game of ping pong,
Going back and forth to events, encounters, and moments in life,
And doing so with different degrees of strife.

In a cloud of thoughts

I find myself becoming drawn up into a cloud,
And which can cloud my judgement,
And fill my mind and heart with contempt.
A cloud of constant thinking,
And which at times makes my gut feel as though it's sinking,
Sinking into a pit of dread,
Where I find myself creating a thread.
A long winding thread of different times,
Moments and experiences difficult to shake and let go of,
Though I also wonder what I may have misread,
And what I can do instead.
I can actually use the cloud as a place to take myself to,
To find quietness, comfort, and peace,
Somewhere where I can approach things with more ease.
To create different visions and ideas,
In the hope to create brighter memories.

Address the mess!

I'm in a right mess,
And where I find I ask myself 'where do I start?'
Sometimes it feels like I'm pulling myself apart.
'Let's start somewhere' I say,
Yes, but am I going the right way?
To uncovering, understanding, and making sense of what has been,
What if I can't handle what is becoming seen?
Well, I'm going to take my time and be kind to myself,
Even if it means becoming messy as I take a delve.

Talk to me

Talk to me, tell me, I'm listening to you.
I'm not going to excuse my fear,
Of what I imagine it would be like if I let you loose,
I want to value and accept you,
Because ultimately you are part of me,
Part of worries, memories, and clarities.
You offer me curiosity, energy, and remedy,
You are a true wonder to me.

Believing

Believing in me,
Is letting me see,
What I can be,
Which brings tremendous glee.
Believing in me counteracts the mental obstruction,
Which can create disruption,
Disruption in being guided by my true potential.
Such potential is essential to embrace,
As I wonder curiously for what else awaits,
And is just the thing I need to have in place.

It's not me, it's you

How could you have done such a thing?! You're to blame!
Blame for something I find difficult to tame,
Where I find myself believing I'm so lame.
It's you who I see in me, in my thoughts and even in dreams,
And I am trying my hardest to move away,
Yet emotionally there is something that has kept me to stay,
Albeit not kept my feelings and emotions at bay.
I imagine it's you too who has issues,
But I feel they are being diffused,
Diffused in a way where I feel emotionally abused,
Finding it difficult to make either of us the accused.

What a let down

I feel disappointed, upset, outraged, and frustrated,
For how I get myself berated.
I know it tends to come from me,
But it started with you having got into me.
I can't say this, think that or feel such a way,
And how I try to keep things at bay.
Over the years what I also know is that I have wealth,
A wealth of information, understanding, and resources,
For me to keep in check my mental health.

The critic in us

Self-criticism is something we may observe,
And which we can learn to preserve,
As a way of preserving ourselves.
Yet what we are also likely to notice,
Is the pressure that comes with the way we measure,
Our sense of self, worth and value.
Who knew that self-criticism can be difficult to shake off,
And if we ask ourselves not to do it again,
Imagine the gain.
But how can we shake it off?
As for many of us it can almost be like breaking off,
Breaking off a part of ourselves which has developed and come to be,
And which can be difficult to flee.
What's in a measure?
Particularly if it makes us miss some of the pleasures,
The wants, the aspirations.
What's needed is admiration,
Admiration of ourselves and others which we are to encourage,
And which is what I see as courage,
Courage for how things need to be,
And which can make us free.
Free to express and positively challenge ourselves,
Surely, that's a kinder way to measure.

Holding on

It may seem inevitable,
That our past will always last,
And which we may find hard to move past,
Creating a cast,
Casting doubt, fear, frustration, envy,
Which can be found in you and me.
The cast can cloud our perceptions, judgments, and actions,
Sometimes a great deal and other times by a fraction.
Our past can create mess,
Mess we may go on to call emotional distress.
Let's not over stress,
As the past can also help us,
Help us take what we want into the present and future.
Instead of the cast it can shed light,
Making things a little bright,
Guiding us to where we want to be,
And where we can say to ourselves, 'that's an important part of me!'

Going back without staying back

We can mentally and emotionally take ourselves,
And connect to past times, experiences, and memories,
Whilst acknowledging the distance and journey we have travelled,
Through our investment, commitment, strive and triumph,
Which has brought us to the present.

Adversities

From different adversities it's possible we have experienced hurt,
And which may mean we have become ever more alert,
Alert not to be emotionally attacked,
Particularly if we have found ourselves not being backed,
Something we notice having lacked.

Conflicted

Conflicted by the pain afflicted,
Which has become depicted,
Depicted in the way we may pull away,
And push ourselves back,
Believing there are a multitude of things we lack.
What has lacked we may never get back,
Yet what we can have, is our own back.

Tension

Being tense can become so intense,
Where parts of our being feel oh so dense.
Carrying an uncomfortable and overbearing weight,
And which can irritate,
Making us feel consumed.
What needs to be resumed,
Is being free to live our true lives,
Doing so, no longer with despise.

Feeling the pressure

Pressure when we try to measure,
Measure ourselves against,
A myriad of challenges, undertakings, and tasks,
And which can at times be a big ask.
The pressure can create a sense of displeasure,
So let's take a refresher,
And set our compass on the things we have made happen,
And which we can treasure.

Worry

I worry about this, I worry about that,
I worry about pretty much everything,
And that's a fact!
The worries can be of different sizes,
And they can also come in different guises.
A worry can set off another worry,
And can lead to preoccupation,
With it bringing about a sense of mental, emotional, and physical
suffocation.
A worry can feel very heavy,
And as though it is with us for what seems like eternity,
Worry is something I see all around me.
Seeing the worries of you, them, and society,
It's clear we all have worries of some degree.
There are worries we may push back,
As well as those we may try to attack.
Whatever the case, the reality is that worry is part of our life story
and history,
And it's through creating opportunity for reflexivity,
Where we are more likely to experience victory.

Let's delve in

Let's delve into what got us here,
The times when we may have shed a tear,
Speaking about a fear.
Fear of not being valued, respected, and loved,
Where we may have felt emotionally shoved,
Shoved into a restricted place,
When life has felt like a race.
Akin to a battle.
It is something we need to dismantle,
To see the fullness of life,
That ultimately requires tremendous strife.

Rejection

Rejection can feel like an injection of emotional pain.
Furthermore, rejection can also involve us rejecting,
Rejecting attitudes, beliefs, and even relationships,
Which is a disservice to us.

Approval

A strong need for approval can make us aloof,
Emotionally distant, disconnected, dejected,
And rejecting towards the whole of our being.
What can be is the approval we can give ourselves,
The openness, opportunity, and expression,
Being attuned, responsive, responsible, and accommodating towards,
The array of necessities,
For the governance we can have,
In living a life that we can call ours.
It is this way of being and navigating the relationship with approval,
That can be more enriching and fulfilling.

I get you

I can feel so alone, so distant,
Feeling hesitant,
Hesitant to be open, to be seen, to be judged.
Am I stupid, absurd, nonsensical?
But no, you do get me.
I know the value of me getting to know myself,
Whilst also knowing that I am not completely alone,
As there are others looking,
Looking for understanding, acceptance, and connection.

Validation

Validation can form the foundation,
For what we need to be seen for,
As we seek love and admiration.
It can have a strong bearing on our self-formation,
And may lead to us needing to engage in self-restoration.

Let's make it work!

'Come on, we can do this.'
Who am I really saying that to?
I'm saying it to me and to you.
Life can become so blue,
Where it can be difficult finding another hue,
And with it, light and brightness,
Yet what we seem to come across is a kind of tightness.
The tightness can be explosive and make us want to burst,
Burst into pieces, as we strive to create a deeper sense of existence.
That time will come, it's imminent,
And what I need from myself is persistence.

Stress

Stress can be something we want to compress,
But which instead can lead to distress.
Bringing about frustration, despair, and tension.
Let it be our mission,
To unpick what is under the stress,
Exploring and navigating what becomes exposed,
Which up until now had remained closed.
Battling with the pains of reality,
Whist trying to claim ourselves,
We exclaim, 'let me be!'

Caught up

Life can feel like a web,
Where we at times become stuck,
Saying, 'this is just my luck!'
How can we help ourselves become unstuck?
Rather than feeling trapped,
We need to see the web as something we can adapt,
Adapt and form into something offering safety, structure, and
containment,
Where we can engage in obtainment and attainment.
The web of life can reflect what we want and need,
Where we can thread in and incorporate what we value and give
heed.

'Nice to meet you!'

Through our engagement with getting to know and meet ourselves,
We have begun the process of coming out of our shells,
It's not easy and takes patience, perseverance, and commitment,
And which can enable us to become more self-confident.
Meeting ourselves can be met with wonder, curiosity, joy, fear,
anxiety, relief,
Whilst also bringing about a sense of disbelief.
Nice to meet you may feel overdue,
Yet what is probable is that it's you being true.

Emotional wounds

Emotional wounds whilst they can heal can leave an impression,
Marking what we have encountered, endured, and battled with.
This can at times make us overprotective of ourselves,
And what we believe we can tolerate and at other times,
Give us more drive and determination to say, 'bring it on!'

Wounded but not defeated

Wounded but not defeated,
By how events and encounters have left us treated.
Seeing how pain has become deep rooted,
Rooted in the pain are the doubts, questions, and frustration,
Of what can seem like condemnation,
Some of which causing great tribulation.
Admiration to our hurt souls,
Which still wants us to live towards our goals,
Acknowledging the deep-rooted turmoil yet still rooting for us,
And which undoubtedly is a plus.

Gratitude

Gratitude can be akin to an attitude of appreciation,
Appreciation of having ourselves,
And the experiences, moments, and memories,
Knowing that no matter what,
We are always going to be there for ourselves.

Feel what's real

Feeling what's real,
Can seem like a big deal,
As we go through our emotions wheel,
Where we try to reel in the way life has been more like a spiel.
It may seem unreal how we have latched on to a way of being,
At the expense of disregarding our emotional being.
By us being real with and in ourselves,
Can be a new path we pave,
And which may have been something we have so desperately craved.
Paving the way is inevitable,
As what we feel is inseparable,
Inseparable to us, others, and the world,
So let's go back to our emotions wheel,
And strike a deal with what is truly of appeal.

Dreams are there for the making

Dreams are there for the making,

And which can also be there for the taking.

We may find ourselves robbed of the opportunity,

To engage with aspirations,

Despite strong determinations.

But who can stop us, when we have that fire in us,

Even when others may say 'stop making a fuss!'

Making a fuss?! We have got this and can do it,

So long as we are prepared to pull through it.

Pull through even if it means us becoming red in hue,

Being passionate about creating a new vision for me and you.

You've got you!

Key ways to promote your mental health and wellbeing

Whether we like it or not, the only person who will always be in our lives is ourselves. It's a given; we can never avoid ourselves. Just think about how our shadows always follow us around. It is not only our shadows; our thoughts, beliefs, and attitudes can also find ways of following us around.

Even though it may not always seem that way, we can choose who we want in our lives and the significance, value, and impact they have. This in turn is reflected in the way we invest in those relationships. Regarding relationships, it is also important for us to identify how we can go about promoting our relationship with ourselves.

For some individuals, a lack of support, encouragement, and guidance from others has led to them believing they only have themselves to depend on. For some others, considering their own needs may seem like unfamiliar territory if for example, they have tended to respond to and prioritise other people and their needs. The same could be said if an individual does not hold value towards themself and therefore disregards what they truly need. Whatever position we find ourselves in, what is fundamental is that just like we tend to expect things from ourselves, we also need to expect things for ourselves.

The following sections explore some of the key ways of ensuring we remain invested in our mental health and wellbeing.

The web of life

Life can, at times, feel rather full on and we may notice we are doing one thing after another. Some of us may be good at, or at least used to, finding ways of effectively juggling and managing different tasks, roles, responsibilities, and commitments which are part of our lives.

Some people genuinely like the busyness of their lives as it can make them feel more focused, motivated, and productive, which can deepen their sense of purpose. This can be true especially if a person believes they are the one who is in control of how they are living their life. Metaphorically speaking, if an individual is spinning themselves more things to do and consequently more of themselves into such things, keeping busy can serve as a distraction and mean they avoid what really needs their time and attention. In addition, a person may become stuck in a particular part of the web of life and end up feeling caught up rather than being able to move around the web with flexibility and adaptability.

By viewing life as a web where we are creating space for all it can bring, it can help in developing perspective of where we are, where we have come from, and where we want to be. The web can also demonstrate the proximity and distance between different areas of life, as well as what may be impacted if we change the way we behave and treat different parts.

The image of a web came to me when I was reflecting on the concept of a person's circles of support. This is where the most inner circle represents the most fundamental aspects of life, such as values, beliefs, and identity. When it comes to the web of life, the centre of the web is the most important part which holds things together and without which it would not be possible for other sections to be created. This inner part in many respects represents the individual themselves as we are the creators of what we engage and interact with in life.

If we find ourselves caught up disproportionately in a certain part of the web of life, it can become difficult to go on creating the web with structure and balance, which is key. Sticking to one part of the web may indicate that we do not give ourselves the opportunity to construct other areas, which may lead to some of our needs being neglected.

What is paramount in both creating and moving to different parts of the web is to have varied and sufficient resources available as and when they are required. An example is when a person feels tired, they can move to a part of the web which offers a resting place. The value in this concept is that more areas can be added including those that can ease the transition from one place to another, in other words, from one area of life to another. Furthermore, an individual does not need to feel caught up by a part no longer serving them as it can be replaced. The purpose of the web is therefore to function in such a way which makes a person feel supported by it.

Undress stress – uncovering the source of our stress

'Argh!!' Does it ever feel like life is not on your side, where it is throwing all sorts of challenges and dilemmas your way?

The truth of the matter is that life can bring about all kinds of stress and we are likely to find some things more stressful than others. Many of us have grappled with some kind of stress and when stress accumulates, it can leave us feeling completely depleted. Because of this, our response to a situation or event may be disproportionate, although we might not recognise it as such until others point it out to us or we have had time to reflect.

Like the way we dress ourselves, where we think about what to wear given the climate and occasion, it can also be helpful to see stress as something that we can make more of a conscious judgement about. Let me give you an exercise. In your mind, go back to the last time you remember feeling stressed. It may have been some time ago or it may be recent. Whichever it is, think back to what could have triggered the stress. Was it completely attributable to the particular event or situation, or could the stress have been triggered by something else, possibly a stressor that you may not have given sufficient attention to? As you look back, imagine yourself slowly, metaphorically speaking, undressing the stress to observe what is underneath it. It could be an accumulation of different issues you have carried with you is making you vulnerable to be reactive rather than responsive to what really needs to be addressed.

Even though a certain amount of stress is necessary and at times vital, we need to ensure we are sufficiently attending to and engaging with a stressor without getting stressed out! Just like the way most of us wear clothes to make us feel comfortable and prepared for the day, we also need to better prepare ourselves in the way we stress. Staying with the clothing analogy, picture yourself on a rather warm summer's day being wrapped in so many layers of clothing that you feel extremely hot, uncomfortable, and irritated. Now what might you be inclined to do? I assume that most of us would take off the extra layers of clothing to be able to go about our day in a more comfortable and manageable way.

It is possible that stress arises from a mix of what is going on currently and what has been going on for some time. In the moment this appears just, though it is ultimately an injustice to ourselves, our emotions, and the situation at hand.

With so many of us trying to balance multiple things in our lives, there is potential for tension to build up. For example, we may be carrying things with us which have not been resolved or responded to in the way they need to be. Even though we may just want to move on and get on with things, to make life as efficient and manageable as possible, the reality is that we cannot completely separate the present from things leading up to it. What is likely to happen is that we find ourselves bringing things from previous encounters that are looking for acknowledgement and expression.

What is therefore conducive is if we ask ourselves what we are really responding to; to unpick what is going on for us that makes us engage in such a way in the present moment. Once we do, we can discern whether now is the time and place to attend to it and if not, what a more optimal way would be. By unpicking and deconstructing what needs more acknowledgement and attention, we can better navigate how much of our personal resources we need to offer. By engaging in the process of mentally "undressing" stress to uncover what is contributing to it, we can be better at re-dressing and therefore re-addressing different situations and encounters.

At-Tension – paying attention to tension

'You seem tense.' Many of us have probably come across such a comment which reflects how life can be taxing, creating pressure and tension in us. Additionally, the more we have going on, the more difficult it can be to find time and space to reflect on and attend to what impacts us, as we may find the demands of life absorbing our attention. Understandably there are a variety of situations which require differing amounts of attention from us. Considering attention as a resource that we give to different things, there is no doubt that over time, we can become under-resourced, with attention creating tension.

Tension, in the different forms it can take, can make us feel stressed and vulnerable as well as bring about feelings of exasperation and possibly despair. Tension may present in a number of ways, including difficulties with mood, sleep, appetite, motivation, and concentration, as well as mental and physical tiredness.

I have learned through training, reading, and research, as well as the different individuals I have worked with that it may be helpful to see tension in three ways: physical, mental, and emotional.

When it comes to physical tension, we may notice stiffness, pain, or discomfort in parts of our bodies which can induce fatigue and restlessness. Mental tension may cause us to feel mentally swamped, impairing our ability to think clearly and make constructive decisions. With emotional tension, we may be carrying unprocessed feelings and emotions which are intolerable and overwhelming. Any one of these types of tension can set off or be set off by one of the others, and they can also be experienced simultaneously. It is only when we step back and take time to assess and evaluate the impact of what we are involved in that we can better understand how to change things so they become more tolerable, purposeful, and engaging,

It may be beneficial to look at some strategies and resources which could be used in managing and potentially navigating the different types of tension.

Regarding physical tension, a body scan can be beneficial. As the name suggests, you scan different parts of your body for tension, starting from the head and slowly working down to the feet, breathing in calmness and breathing out tension.

A massage can also be a source of relief, though I am aware that some people, for valid reasons, do not feel comfortable with physical touch and can still feel connection with activities such as Reiki which is a form of energy healing.

By engaging in exercise, whether it is high or low intensity such as running, cycling, walking, swimming, or yoga, this can alleviate physical tension as well as promote focus and clarity, and be mentally restoring.

Mentally taking ourselves to a place which we associate with calmness, peace, and tranquillity can be a powerful practice and is something which can be readily available and accessible to us. It may be a place we have physically been to, or it may be a collection of places or things we associate with mental restoration. It may be clear to imagine what we need, and we can also add more resources to the place as we encounter different events contributing to mental tension. In addition, mindfulness practices such as meditation can help us connect with the present moment and let go of the tiresome happenings in our minds.

Writing things down can also help create mental space and distance, promote reflexivity, as well as aiding memory. Creating a checklist can help us identify, keep note of, track, and prioritise tasks and related actions, promoting our sense of agency and self-efficacy.

When it comes to emotional tension, journaling can be a way of making sense of our thoughts and feelings where through the process of writing, we begin to process what going on in our emotional lives.

Talking to significant others where possible about what's going on for us and the emotional impact it is having can help us feel understood and supported. Engaging in therapy can also be a great way to attend to, explore, as well as navigate our emotional landscape, where there can be regular and protected space to offload ourselves from what makes us feel tense.

I imagine readers have heard of some if not all these resources and may have engaged in them too. What is important to note is that these ways of assessing and working with different types of tension are pivotal to self-care and I would encourage all of us to use them on an ongoing basis.

'What are you sensing?' Making the most of our senses

'Wow that smells good!' We may have said this about the tantalising scent of a meal we are presented with. Or it could have been when trying on different perfumes or becoming aware of a fragrance as someone passes us. The sense of smell can create all types of feelings and sensations such as exuberance, uplift, and arousal, and there is no doubt regarding the power of our senses.

But what about times when we find ourselves senseless when it comes to connecting with our senses? Can you remember a time when you have been so preoccupied with the demands of life or felt so overwhelmed that it has left you disconnected with yourself and your surroundings? I am sure we have all had times when we have not been as "sense-full" as we would like to have been. It could also be that we connect with some senses more than others, which could be down to biological and physiological factors. Not connecting with some of our senses may also be tied to loss, where we have lost a part of ourselves. Speaking of loss, there may be a lack of stimulation or mental and emotional nourishment in a person's life which means they do not have a full sense of who they are and what they need.

When it comes to our senses there can be a high degree of nostalgia, whereby an expression, a sound, a taste, a smell, a sight, or a physical impression can take us to a former time and place. I believe there are a lot of parallels between how we are the directors of our lives and how we can redirect ourselves to times and places which hold personal meaning and significance. One way we can do this is through our senses, so let's put that into motion. In your mind, replay one of the most captivating moments of your life. It may have been a moment from quite some time ago, or a more recent encounter. What do you cherish most about that moment? In other words, what stands out when you think back to it? What you may have noticed standing out could be a result of your senses. For instance, the sound of waves, the warmth and brightness of the sun, the laughter of loved ones, the smell and taste of an enjoyable meal, the feeling of wearing a particular outfit. You could say it was your senses inviting you back to such a remembered occasion.

It is our senses which make certain things appealing but they can also work in the opposite direction, whereby our senses deter us. Our senses can act as a survival mechanism, being reactive towards stimuli and situations which are perceived as posing a threat. It is therefore of great importance to acknowledge the different roles, functions, and impact our senses have in our lives, so I invite you to connect with your senses in ways which makes sense to you.

Get a grip! The power of grounding

'Get a grip!' 'Get a hold of yourself!' We may say such things to ourselves when we are unable to connect with our presence in the present moment. Following on from the previous section regarding our senses, I would say it is even more important to bring our senses to the forefront of our awareness. Difficulty experiencing connection with the present can be triggered by a number of different factors. For example, it can be linked to the need to create safety wherein a previous event or encounter posed a threat to a person's survival. They may not have been able to prevent or escape from a threat in that moment, leading them to feel stuck in it. We can also feel burdened and tied down by our past or what we anticipate happening in the future. This can cause us to find it difficult to connect with the present, despite it being the time we have the most control over and which offers us the greatest potential for change. This way of engaging, or shall I say disengaging with ourselves and the world can make us feel disconnected and even isolated. It is possible that we end up having a passive role in our lives, rather than being active and self-governing. At times this is probably due to the need to feel in control from a time when we felt out of control. However, I do believe that just as we acknowledge how invaluable and enriching the role of our senses are, with understanding, support, and encouragement, we can begin to allow ourselves to access resources that help us connect with the present.

Here's a scenario that most of us have probably experienced: imagine finding yourself waking up from a bad dream. The dream could have felt very real and vivid. It could have been a one-off dream causing distress or it could be a recurring one which you feel trapped by. The reality is that life can also feel like a bad dream given the uncertainty and instability that it can bring. I believe we need to give ourselves something to hold onto that helps us feel grounded.

The good thing about grounding is that anything can be used in order for us to experience a stronger connection with the present. From touching a physical object, looking at a focal point in our surroundings, listening to a sound, smelling a scent, the choices are limitless. Over time we may be able to engage in such a practice with more ease and can ultimately find the process enriching. Through using different senses we can become more in touch with ourselves and the external world, with our senses becoming an anchor.

Let's put one of our senses into practice. You may have heard of the term, "finding your feet". I invite you to place your feet firmly on the ground, making a conscious effort to notice the different parts of your feet and how they feel being supported. If at first you find this difficult, try applying a bit of pressure whilst exercising gentleness. It may be a good idea to begin with a part of the foot where you feel some sensation, working your way from that area until you experience fuller contact.

Yes, we may at times encounter a sense of being lost or out of touch with ourselves and by "finding our feet", we can create a stronger connection between what is part of us and what is part of our environment. By doing so we can be where we actually need to be, living life with more purpose, engagement, and fulfilment.

Getting connected

'Getting connected?' Some of us may read this and think getting connected means having access to WIFI and the internet. Yes, that could be part of the picture, however I am sure from reading previous sections of this book you can appreciate there are a multitude of resources and ways we can live a healthy, purposeful, and fulfilling life. Getting connected involves a feeling of captivation and enrichment, not only with the place we are physically in but also with the mental and emotional space we occupy.

This may seem like more of an aspiration, a dream which appears far-fetched, and we may have our individual reasons for believing something is out of reach. How is it possible to experience total contentment and complete connection in these different aspects of our being? Well, let me put it another way. Why is it that so many of us strive to find and hold down a job? A big part of it is likely to do with the financial gains and security that comes with a paid job, as well as other opportunities that it could offer. For example, it could be about the structure, routine, discipline, purpose, and professional investment we have towards ourselves and how that investment may also serve others in our lives. It could also involve our need to feel valued, recognised, appreciated, and supported by people in our workplace. You may have identified other reasons and in any case, we have a tendency not to engage in something if there is no gain at some level, and therefore no connection. Undoubtedly there are things which do not completely suit us, yet the positives outweigh the negatives, as long as we recognise the physical, mental, and emotional connection within aspects of an endeavour. Staying with the example of a job, think about the connection between getting physically ready for it through the clothes we wear, getting mentally prepared to ensure we can sufficiently concentrate, and maintaining the emotional capacity to manage the pressures and taxing encounters which are inevitable as we engage with the workplace. All this is needed to feel more able to approach situations and interactions with more confidence, composure, responsivity, and compassion.

Now, in order to do well in the workplace, we also need to be doing well outside of it. When it comes to doing well, I would like to draw your attention back to the notion of experiencing connection. Using the workplace as an analogy, I anticipate it would be easier for readers to imagine if they are working, previously working or would like to be doing so in the future. I can also appreciate how for some the workplace may not be the most optimum environment so it is OK to think of another commitment or regular engagement you may have. Visualise there being a large window that you walk over to and open. As you open it, you see yourself connected with all of you and all aspects of where you are. What might that look like for you? Well, it is very likely that it will look different depending on the person observing and what is being seen. For some, they may see nature, hues of green, flowers blooming, birds, and other wildlife. For others they may see musical instruments, certain objects, or people. There may be a certain vastness to the space, or the space may be quite defined, protected with some sort of boundary. Irrespective of how the space looks, it is more about how it can be connected with.

Guess what? This is life! Sometimes in our imagination we see the ideal we want to have in our lives. It is also something I invite my clients to engage in when I ask them the following: 'Imagine waking up tomorrow morning and finding yourself feeling more content. How would feeling content look? How could you tell you were feeling such a way? What would you see, notice?' Engaging in this type of self-reflection is in itself a reflection of the things we need to have in our lives. So, if you continue visualising the window and what you see though it, there may be some things which are closer, some things which take up more space, and some things that can only be seen from a distance, yet which are also important. All of these things and their positionality, size, and proportion are fundamental to how connected and sustained we feel. There may be times and events which lead to us moving or removing certain objects and entities. So, the questions remains … what do you see or want to see as you look out of the window of life?

This is my kind of music!

Have you ever heard a song playing where you find yourself saying, 'That's my song!' It might be when you're out socially or at an event. It may be overheard when passing someone who is playing music, or you may turn the radio on and it's the song you remember dancing to or having some memory around. It might also be a song on your playlist that you actively look for or when it randomly plays you feel an immense sense of captivation. You may also play music depending on the kind of activity you are engaged in, for example going for a run, working out, cooking, cleaning, writing, doing some self-care, or as a way to relax. Music can also be used as something that boosts mood, promotes connection, and helps us process encounters, as well as be a form of self-expression.

If we ask what is it about ourselves that leads us to connect with a song, what would we say? I am aware that things such as the sounds of certain instruments, the tone, rhythm, beat, lyrics, or the artist's voice can play a part in how we relate to a piece of music. The presence of such impetuses can make other things such as our thoughts and worries fade into the background. Conversely, a song can also capture exactly what is going on in our mental, emotional, and physical beings.

Let me give you a scenario. Imagine hearing a song which you may or may not have heard before, yet when you start paying attention to it, you notice it is communicating something about you. It may even be something that up until this moment you have not particularly given much attention to. It could be around a moment where you have felt sadness, guilt, pain, anger, loneliness, fear, a sense of feeling lost, stuck, joyful, or content.

If you were to compose a song where there were distinctive elements to it, what would they be? What would you want to name the song? Would there be potential for the song to be part of an album if there are numerous events and experiences you intend to capture? Or is it more about how one song can be an acknowledgement of what you have challenged and which, metaphorically speaking, you may want to replay. Playing our own tunes can help us encapsulate and integrate key and defining moments into the soundtrack of life.

Get a move on! Creating expression through movement

'Get a move on!' Most of us have probably heard ourselves or someone else saying this to communicate a sense of urgency and the need to speed things up. This does not necessarily need to involve anything too intensive but illustrates the importance of incorporating more movement in our lives. Some of us may have a set activity or activities as part of our routine. It could be something like going for a walk, stretching as we get out of bed, or doing a "power pose" in front of the mirror as we prepare for our day.

There are so many ways we may already have movement in our lives, some which we may not be conscious of. Let's give ourselves some time to think more about that. Think about what you have done today up until now. Reading this, you are definitely awake, so I imagine you have moved around, including the physical movement of picking up and opening this book. Undoubtedly some movements are bigger than others and some may be in sequence, for example when getting ready in the mornings. Some movements last longer, if for instance we need to travel to another place. Movements can be relaxing, balancing, and restorative such as yoga; they can also be uplifting and energising like dancing.

Are you able to identify what movements you do more often? If so, what does each of these movements do for you? Do you feel you have enough movement in your day, or is more needed? If so, what kinds of movement?

Just as physical movement is important for us, so is mental and emotional movement. By physically moving from one space to another, we give ourselves the opportunity to create a shift in how we think and feel.

Let's, figuratively speaking, take ourselves for a walk. Imagine walking somewhere where you can immerse yourself. As you imagine yourself walking, you may notice a pace or a kind of rhythm in the way you move. You may also notice how different parts of your body feel, from your legs up to your arms and hands, your shoulders, back, neck, and head. You may sense different types and degrees of movement in each part of your physical being. As you become more aware of the different movements in different parts of your body, you may subsequently notice a sensation, feeling, and even further motion which may create "movement" in your state of mind or perspective.

It is not just about outward movements. Engaging in actively scanning our bodies to discern where we need to create some internal release, movement, and motion can create expression where incremental movements can help us tune into and connect with different parts of ourselves.

What are you looking at? The significance of what we set our sights and minds on

You may have described yourself or another person in a way that defines the level of pessimism or optimism an outlook has. Also, you have likely heard the analogy of a glass half full or half empty. Is your attitude towards life akin to the glass? I would describe myself as someone who sees both the fullness and emptiness life can provide the glass. I also see the glass as representing ourselves, which makes it possible to pay attention to how much life is in us.

In life it is likely that the glass contains a combination of resources that will fluctuate as we encounter and respond to different challenges and stressors. This can create an imbalance, so there will be a need to "fuel up" and "recharge". It is valuable to think about what can "fill" and "give life" to what has become deficient.

It could be that there have been things missing in our lives, including things we might ourselves have deserted. Or we may have set our sights high in order to attain what we want and have the determination to make these things happen. Therefore, we need to ensure we have the necessary resources. There are different factors which can impact how resourced a person feels, some external and some internal, which can involve a person's self-belief and self-worth. Just like we are multi-faceted beings, so too are our experiences, responses, learnings, and attitudes which are likely to make up the cocktail of life. So, if I ask you, 'What is in your cocktail of life?' What would you say? Are there certain "liquids" which are golden, rich, and with a distinct flavour?

Let's look at things from another angle. Imagine you being able to see inside of yourself. Are there certain parts of you that feel fuller than other parts? If so, can you identify where some of it comes from? For instance, engaging in an activity that is related to a hobby, passion, or which involves self-care? Does that help keep you held together? What about parts which may not appear as full? What kinds of resources do they need? How we look at something can reflect how we are looking at ourselves. I therefore encourage you to look for what you already have and find out how you can determine and seek what is still needed.

Where do you come from? Exploring our thoughts and beliefs. Are they a service or a disservice to us?

'I'm so silly.' 'I'm rubbish.' 'I always mess up!' 'Everything is my fault!' Let's not make it all about us. What I mean is that it is very unlikely that a situation is entirely our doing. As human beings we have a tendency of wanting to exercise a sense of control and governance around our lives. Where the difficulty lies however, is that we cannot be in complete control over our thoughts because they are partly influenced by external factors which impact our views and beliefs.

Let's spend some time looking more closely at our thoughts. I invite you to think about the most recent thought you noticed having about yourself, others, or the world. How much weight do you give that thought? If that kind of thought has come before, what has led to you having the thought? Was it brought on by certain factors and if so, what were they? Do you tend to spend time entertaining the thought, or do you try to disregard it?

It could be that we are so used to a thought that it becomes an automatic way of perceiving, conceptualising, and subsequently confronting different aspects of our lives. Over time we learn to trust what we think, perceive, believe, and do. Not only are we more likely to place trust in what we believe, we are also likely to believe those we trust, whether it is family, friends, or other individuals we have a significant relationship with or hold in high regard. As well as trusting we are also likely to value the person and therefore value what they believe, including their way of thinking. This can also be part of our quest in seeking guidance, direction, and certainty. Furthermore, another person's views and beliefs can become such that we incorporate them into our thinking and belief system. In some ways taking something served to us can help us to bypass and navigate our anxieties around uncertainty, though can also convey a lack of trust in ourselves or a need to please others, which may not serve us well. Some thoughts may contribute to rigidity, a sense of feeling stuck or dissatisfaction, and may conversely lead to us feeling frustrated and even resentful.

If we are more trusting of what others say and believe, there could be a disparity between the views of others and what we believe from what our thoughts communicate to us. By examining our thoughts and understanding where they come from and what they inform, we can know more about what purpose they are serving. By doing so, we can decide whether they are doing a just or an unjust service.

What's in a word? The words we expose ourselves to

It may be a single word, phrase, term, or expression; it may be something we have seldom heard or encountered more frequently. You may agree when I say words can have the potential to carry a lot of weight and power. Verbal expressions can have underlying meanings and messages or be intended to provoke a reaction and can communicate all sorts of information. We are both the listeners and speakers of different words, so it is important to tune into the presence and absence of words and the impact they have.

Thinking about words, terms, and phrases you have heard including those you have said yourself, what bearing have they had in your life? What has been positive about them? How about times when they have been more negative in tone? What impact have they had? Now, bring your attention to the absence of certain words. How has it been not to hear them? Have there been times when you have wanted to hear such words from others as well as yourself?

The words we use can be a reflection of our reality and the way we see the world, others and ourselves. Words can also be used to reframe and reconstruct our perspective. A prime example of this is self-talk, where we may encourage ourselves to engage in internal dialogue, which is more self-accepting and compassionate. Self-affirming words and phrases can help us see that we are worthy and recognise our need to feel understood, valued, and encouraged. The good thing about it is that as it comes from us, we can exercise control over it.

We do not need to seek affirmation from anyone else, though that is not to say we need to disregard other people and what they are saying. It is about ensuring we offer ourselves ample opportunity to see ourselves for all we are. Each of us can ultimately decide which words we allow ourselves to hold on to, which stick, and which words have less significance.

In relation to words, it may also be helpful to understand when it is the most constructive time to take on a more active engagement with what we are exposing ourselves to. Thinking about yourself, is it in the morning when you need a boost? As the day progresses and there is more you need to get through?

Could it be before going to bed where a few words about how you got through the day can offer appreciation and restoration? For some of us, hearing encouraging words is something we can embrace whereas for others writing and seeing words is more nurturing. The final word from me is that we use words with care and consideration, both to ourselves and others.

Removing self-doubt, is that what it's all about?

'Do you really see yourself being able to do this?' 'What makes you think you can do it?' 'Don't set yourself up to fail!' 'You'll embarrass yourself.' These self-statements are examples of the messages we may give ourselves when we experience self-doubt. I believe there are countless reasons we may doubt ourselves and that it shows up in our lives in different ways. Entangled in the doubt might be fear, uncertainty, and perceived barriers which may make taking action appear futile or insignificant. Doubt can also be about a lack of self-belief and trust, as well as a lack of encouragement and support we offer ourselves or get from others. The truth is that we have all had very different life experiences, with gains and losses. Such moments create a marker of what we think we can achieve in addition to us questioning whether something is worth taking on. Furthermore, we are likely to assess and judge the extent to which a course of action involves risk or puts us or a part of our lives at stake.

Self-doubt could indicate that we need to gain a deeper understanding of whether something really is worthwhile, or even whether it is something we truly want. We may think we want something because other people or society make us feel as though we want it.

So, what might be invaluable is to ask, 'what is the self-doubt all about?' Let me pose another question to you: can self-doubt ever be a relevant and necessary response?

The answer could be yes if we view self-doubt as a form of self-protection, preservation, as well as promotion. If we anticipate a situation having the potential to create significant risk to ourselves and our survival, self-doubt can make us reassess the situation. Can you think of a time when you doubted yourself, in other words, doubted what you could take on? The reality is that we are more likely to say we doubt ourselves without really looking into what might make doubt the right thing for us to exercise.

One of the most important and helpful aspects of doubt that we develop in relation to ourselves and the outside world is that it can help us look at the resources that govern our capacity and capability as well as how important the particular task is. We can ask ourselves whether it is something we really want and need to do, and if so, assess what we need to give ourselves in undertaking it.

Connected with doubt may be a difficulty in recognising past achievements because if we take note of them, we could understand how those moments may have had elements of doubt involved. If we give ourselves the opportunity to look at such times, we may be able to identify how we navigated the doubt.

And finally, another source of doubt could be associated with doubting our sense of worth. We may ask ourselves, 'Am I worthy of having such a thing in my life?' Can this really happen for me?' It is therefore of great importance to identify the source as well as the type of doubt we hold. Is it about understanding what we value, what we need in order to make something we value come to fruition, or is it about the value we give ourselves?

It's a child's world

It is probably fair to imply that the worldview each of us holds has in many ways been coloured by our experiences growing up. Our earlier experiences can form the impression we create about ourselves, others, and the world, which we are likely to go on to use and apply in subsequent interactions. Prior insights can pave the way for how we relate to future environments, situations, and encounters. Our current responses can therefore reflect how we have taken on and brought into the present our former learnings and understandings.

Prior experiences can be something that we find difficult to create an alternative path from even when it means that carrying on the same path can lead to difficult and possibly undesired outcomes. So, what happens when we find ourselves staying on the same track and repeating the past? What I mean by that is when we are encountering something in the present, we may tend to revert back to past experiences as something is evoked in us telling us to "stay put", to stay with what is familiar.

Despite what may appear as something familiar and something we understand when we are confronted with something resembling the past, it may not be helpful to respond in the same way now. I'm by no means implying that we need to do the complete opposite, although doing the complete opposite can work at certain times depending on what it is that we want to make happen.

Reflecting on what we are more inclined to do given the past, we can use it to understand the response that is necessary and needed in the here and now.

What may make it easier for us to contemplate doing things differently is to say to ourselves, 'Would I listen to a child telling me what to do?' The answer is probably no. How can we as adults listen to a child giving us advice? Where they are is very different to where we are now and not informed by the many experiences we have had over our lives. Even when it seems as though not much has changed or happened, I believe that can be more of a reflection of instances we have felt stuck.

The reality is that there are going to be differences, some of which may be subtle, yet we need to find a different way to engage and interact with the current situation.

What I invite you to do is imagine the younger you, being in front of the now adult you. As you do, I encourage you to listen to what the younger you is saying. It could be that you were met with encounters posing their own challenges so how you responded at the time was aiding.

As well as being caring and understanding towards our younger selves, we also need to demonstrate such things towards our adult selves with regard to what it is we need in the present.

Pick up after yourself! Bringing past personal triumphs into the present

'I've failed.' 'I'm sorry your application has been unsuccessful.' 'Keep up the good work!' You may have encountered such statements which are undoubtedly a reflection of how different aspects of life are about performance and achieving. This can ultimately create a certain level of expectation and associated pressure, which may sometimes be unrealistic and even unhelpful. What it can also involve is thinking about doing well without knowing exactly how. What is significant is what we have needed in order to do well before – in other words the importance of reflecting on and taking account of our past triumphs and successes.

It seems as though we are conditioned into believing that we always need to be going forwards but sometimes we are met with uncertainty and unpreparedness.

Conversely, if we were to mentally go "backwards", we can reflect on and track the steps we took then which led us to a particular outcome. The following can promote such reflection: –

'Just because I knew what I wanted, that may not have meant that I knew exactly what to do to make it happen.'

'How did I come to know that some actions required more time and more effort from me physically, mentally, and emotionally?'

'If I did not know the exact actions I needed to take, how open was I to learning what more or what else was required? For example, allowing myself to develop certain skills or speaking with or consulting certain people?'

'How did I allow myself to learn from times things did not work the way I wanted or anticipated? How did I find the strength and courage to persevere?'

It may be that we have not always allowed ourselves the time and opportunity to reflect. Maybe now is actually a good time to do so as we pause, giving more thought and understanding around such moments.

What I do know is that although there may be times when we feel held back by our past, we can also use our past to offer ourselves insight, wisdom, tools, and resources. By looking at the past we can ask ourselves what we want to take hold of and carry forward. It is a question I ask my clients as it enables them to see where they are and track the things which have got them to certain places and points in their lives, including how they have navigated different obstacles.

What's more, by going back to the way events and actions have contributed to our sense of triumph, this can itself foster feelings of inspiration, courage, and purpose.

When I think of the different journeys we take in life, I sometimes find it helpful to view it as a train journey. At times life can make us stop in our "tracks" but if we look back at the tracks we have laid down, some may be more stable and solid than others, yet all are vital in keeping our journey going. We can use the tracks as something we can build on to enable the journey to continue, recognising that it was the things we put down in our past that has meant we have arrived at the place we are at today.

Give it back! The value of giving

It is possible that you have come across the saying "give and take" because just as it is necessary for us to have the opportunity to receive, we also find it necessary to give. Each of us have different reasons for giving and sometimes we can actually end up receiving something too.

Let's take a closer look at giving. You might remember times you have been a giver, or you might be contemplating engaging in an act of giving. Sometimes it can be difficult to pinpoint specific acts of giving yet I believe every one of us has been in a position of giving, even if we ourselves are not aware of it. An instance of giving might be giving our time, attention, skills, knowledge, or wisdom, and by doing so, we offer support and understanding. I believe a big part of giving comes down to the beliefs, views, and values we hold. The act of giving can offer us purpose, focus, and drive, enabling us to develop passion and commitment in investing in what is of value and significance to us. You can say it promotes the way we connect with ourselves through others and society.

Let me pose the following questions to you: –

- How are you or have been giving?
- What have you received from the act of giving?
- Do you actively try to give? If so, what makes you do so?

By bringing our intentions around giving to the forefront of our awareness, we can acknowledge the impact our actions can have both in the present and possibly even in the future. We can therefore foresee ways we would like to exert our presence in this world and the impact we believe it can have.

When thinking about giving, it may also be helpful to recall times you have been the receiver of someone else's giving. How did you feel about the act of their giving?

How did it make you feel about the person? How did it make you feel about yourself?

You may have felt appreciation towards the other person and viewed yourself as someone who the other person values. The person's act of giving may have consequently, led to you believing that you matter. Now let's turn the tables round by thinking about the impact your giving can have. For some, it can really be a lifeline, a helping hand that offers hope. Given the broad range of difficulties around us, it is always a good time for us to be giving.

'That's very kind of you.' Bringing compassion into our interactions

What is the kindest thing you remember ever saying or having done for someone?
What is the kindest thing you have said or done for yourself?
What made you say or do it? How do you feel now thinking about that time?

'What's with all the questions?' some of you may be thinking. My intention is to evoke the memory, experience, and possibly an image which you may associate with a time where kindness was present. By inviting you to think about such an occasion, it may help you discern the role and impact kindness has had in your life.

What I have come to realise is that there is a tendency for us to be kinder to others than to ourselves. We are likely to convey kindness in different ways and it is our way of offering understanding, support, and of being there for a person. I would say that kindness is something most of us are socialised to enact in our lives, particularly around social and interpersonal interactions, and we therefore may see kindness as a quality we need to possess and pass on to others. With such an emphasis on kindness towards others, I believe it is just as important to demonstrate kindness to ourselves.

Let's now bring our attention to compassion because when I think of compassion, I see it as kindness combined with passion – "Kinpassion". If we are passionate about being kind, it is also important that we feel passionate about connecting on an emotional level with others as well as ourselves. If I was to ask you to look back at a relationship or interaction which you see as supportive, what would you say enabled it to become that way? It is possible that compassion played a role and there was the presence of understanding, validation, and acceptance, as well as kindness.

What I also see in the word compassion is how being there at an emotional level, we are in many ways being a companion.

Time for a few more questions. In your mind, take yourself back to a time when you needed to be that kind, compassionate person to yourself. What would you want to say to yourself? What would the then you have wanted or maybe even needed to hear? Are there any current situations where you believe demonstrating self-compassion can potentially provide a source of support and convey kindness towards yourself? Are there certain responses, gestures, or acts that you would want from and for yourself?

How to reap from sleep

'Any minute now.' I say this whenever I find myself tossing and turning but no matter how tired I am, I still find it difficult to get to sleep. I know I'm not the only one who has experienced difficulties with sleep as I have had countless conversations about sleep with many individuals, both in my personal and professional life. I have read a lot on the topic and have been open to trying a variety of practices to see if it can become any easier to get off to sleep. There are however times when I do fall asleep rather effortlessly without consciously doing anything, yet on the whole I have quite a challenging relationship with sleep.

For many of us, maybe more so at particular times, it can be difficult to switch off from the day, either because we have had so much to deal with, or we think we have not done as much as we would have hoped to. Furthermore, by not sleeping, we are avoiding and pushing back the following day and there may be different reasons for us doing so. I know there have been times when I have been awake, checking the time and thinking to myself, 'time is passing, and you aren't any closer to getting off to sleep.' When the morning has come, I have felt extremely tired and unprepared which has made me want to avoid the day even more.

How can our dilemma with sleep be overcome? The irony is that I usually look forward to going to sleep, even though I can't say for certain whether I will have a restful sleep. Over the years I have discovered how important it is to experience a sense of readiness for falling asleep and this is something I want to share with you.

As I get into bed and settle in, I sense the pillow stably and comfortably being able to hold my head and neck. I also sense my mattress carrying the weight of my body.

My duvet is a layer of protection and a buffer from all the events of the day. I say to myself that I can trust that I will be held and supported by all of these things to feel more at ease with getting off to sleep. What's more is that just like turning off the lights in a room you leave, I mentally try turning off my thoughts by telling myself that the morning is a better time to think about them, when I am more able to engage with them. All I need to think about now is easing different parts of my being to settle in and tell myself that the night is here for me to get the rest I need. Even if I have not had a particularly eventful day, I will still remind myself that sleep might make it easier for me to get what I want done the next day and that I need to put my anxieties to rest.

I wish you all a sleep-full night.

Feel what's real

The title might sound like the name of a song or a motivational speech, yet how often do we find ourselves fully tuning into our feelings? Despite the reality that our emotions can be uncomfortable to feel, if we create space for their expression, becoming more tolerating and accepting of them, this can itself create a sense of relief. The relief can be like sensing physical tension, pain, or discomfort in a part of our body. By noticing and attending to that part of our physical being, we may begin to feel less hurt and, as the hurt begins to lessen, we can feel more at ease in our bodies.

At times it may seem easier to ignore certain feelings, possibly as a way of avoiding and protecting ourselves as it may be something we are unfamiliar with, and it is the unknown that we find a threat. However, the more we try to escape our feelings, the more we are likely to feel disconnected and out of touch with the richness of our encounters and experiences and ultimately ourselves.

I'm not saying that we need to force ourselves to feel everything as when exposing ourselves to our feelings, we may find it overwhelming, confusing, and scary. Sometimes feeling what we genuinely feel requires us to be kinder and gentler towards ourselves when approaching the emotional aspects of our experiences.

Even though we have feelings and emotions, we cannot be at the complete mercy of them. If we were, we may end up feeling caught up and trapped in our inner worlds. This in turn creates difficulty relating to and navigating the outside world, which is also important to get a "feel" for. Like most things, it's all about balance. So, part of feeling what is real involves us understanding and balancing what we can tolerate and accept, as well as recognising what we want to develop a closer and richer connection with.

'Talk to me.' Tuning into our emotions

'I don't want to feel you. Go away!' I wonder if any of us always appreciates our emotions. It is fair to say that we can feel and experience different things by our feelings, which in turn can influence how we feel towards them. Furthermore, our emotions try to communicate something to us and the more we try to fight them off, the more they will find alternative ways of getting through to us. Therefore, it is important to understand our relationship with emotions to be able to understand what makes us take a certain position towards them.

Let me pose the following questions to you: –

- How were emotions viewed when you were growing up? Were they acknowledged, validated, encouraged, discouraged, criticised, disregarded, deflected?
- Have you ever felt at the mercy of an emotion? Have you felt stuck, trapped, defenceless, or consumed by a strong feeling?
- Have emotions created a connection or more of a disconnection?

- Have you felt supported or let down when expressing emotions?

You may have said yes to some or even all the above. The reality is that we all at one time or another are likely to experience inner conflict with both our emotions and how we feel towards them.

We can also experience conflict when we find ourselves feeling different emotions at the same time, for example anxiety and relief. Conversely, feeling two opposing emotions can bring about a sense of curiosity, openness, and insight which can help in unravelling the intricacies of the way we related to different encounters.

Let's put that into practice. I would like to invite you to think of a time when you have felt two opposing emotions. What were those emotions? What were they saying to you? If you cannot recall experiencing two emotions simultaneously, imagine feeling two emotions that you have previously felt on their own and bring them together. What feelings arise in you? My reasoning behind asking readers to engage in such an exercise is so that we can witness, tolerate, and even embrace our emotions because they are ultimately a part of us. By rejecting an emotion, we are essentially rejecting a part of ourselves and our experience.

Let me put it another way. How many times have you found yourself appreciating what you have after encountering some kind of adversity or struggle, no matter how small or insignificant that thing may be?

Here's an acronym I have put together for the word emotion.

E – emotions can be Eerie, Entrapping, Expressive, as well as create Ease.

M – emotions can create Movement and Motion and can Make a lot of sense!

O – emotions can sometimes Oscillate in intensity and bearing.

T – emotions can be Tricky, Tormenting, and Telling.

I – emotions can be Insightful.

O – emotions help us Observe Ourselves and Our environment.

N – emotions can feel Nerve-racking, a Nuisance, and can also be Nuanced and Nice.

What do your emotions say to you?

Yours is better than mine- our tendency to engage in self-comparison

What is it that we truly want? How do we measure it? Is it to do with a sense of injustice where it seems as though others have more than what we think we have?

It is not only our tendency to compare ourselves and our lives with others; we are also likely to compare ourselves with the person we once were or wanted to be, or even the person other people wanted us to be. Doubt, confusion, and a sense of feeling lost can creep in if we notice there being a stark contrast between how we see ourselves and how we can be.

Let's look at a fictitious character, George to look more closely at self-comparison. George is in his forties and has found it difficult getting on the "ladder of life", whilst seeing other people move and progress. To George, others appear to have established themselves professionally, are in relationships, some have children, and have a big social circle. No matter how much George tries to reach for some of these things, he feels further and further away from them. Over the years George has become quite withdrawn, and in some ways is more of an observer of life. He sees other people actively engaging in life, whereas he is missing out and very much feels lonely and isolated. George has found himself feeling regretful, angered, and resentful towards himself and society. George cannot take this endless mental and emotional battle any longer and decides that he needs to speak to someone. This also has its own difficulties as George does not want to feel like a burden nor experience judgement. He anticipates that the struggles he is encountering may not be understood and that the person he talks to may not "get him", thinking this risks creating even more of a divide between him and the world. George goes back and forth in his mind about whether he should speak to anyone about his difficulties before deciding to call a friend whom he has not spoken to for some time. As George allows himself to open up, he is taken aback when he hears his friend conveying admiration towards him in being so forthcoming. To his surprise, the friend also opens up, sharing with George some of his own struggles which up until now George had no idea about.

Over time, George begins to see that there were times in his life when circumstances did not make it easy for him to do what he wanted. What's more is that George could also see how there were moments when it was difficult for him to discern and navigate between what he thinks he wants and what he really wants. George also reflected on how he has engaged with certain things in meaningful and significant ways, seeing what is actually present in his life rather than striving to be anywhere but where he currently is. Making self-comparisons can be helpful if we use them to see what we have been able to offer ourselves and make happen, rather than if we did not engage in such acts and processes. We can also use it to see how we made decisions according to our beliefs, values, needs, as well as the resources we had available at the time.

Conversely, if we believe that other people have it better than us, there may also be moments when we believe that we don't have it as bad as others and we do not really have anything to complain about. It may lead to invalidating or disregarding what has contributed to our disappointment or distress, where we may lose touch with ourselves, as well as others and society as a whole. By engaging in self-comparison in such a way we are likely to create disconnection, isolation, and ultimately further distress from which we may experience more pain. What might help restore connection is reminding ourselves that like others, we too have things which are positive as well as things we grapple with. By engaging in this type of self-comparison, we are able to better understand, relate to, and recognise what is meeting our needs and more conducive and optimal ways of exploring and addressing what it is we are seeking.

'What a relief!' The importance of unburdening ourselves from unmanageable expectations

'I need to do this; I need to do that'. Life involves us performing, striving to get things done, to achieve and excel, even though we may not always realise what is making us give so much attention to some of these things. What can happen as a result is that we expect more from ourselves; the more we do, the more there is to do. Why is it that we can be so demanding of ourselves? I don't believe that's a straightforward question to answer. I do know that what we expect of ourselves reflects the roles, responsibilities, and commitments we take on. Furthermore, we may have reasons and motivations for what we expect of ourselves. For example, we may want to feel valued, respected, and loved. What is also important to recognise is that our expectations can instil belief and trust in ourselves, making us feel more confident in our abilities as well as our wants. Like most other things, it involves balancing what is a reasonable and valuable expectation to have, and what may hinder what we need to sufficiently attend to and engage in.

So, what happens when expectations become overwhelming and burdensome? What if they become a source of frustration or resentment, or where we end up feeling stuck? I have listened to countless accounts of people expressing how they have found different expectations which they have placed on themselves, or which may have been placed by others in their lives. The more we try to live life according to such expectations the more we may lose touch with what we truly want. If we constantly have expectations pushing us in another direction creating tension and conflict, this can lead to us failing to give attention, commitment, and investment to what truly matters to us.

It is plausible that the very act of contemplating creating change around our self-expectations can itself seem like an unmanageable expectation. So, the question remains; do we want to accept what we expect of ourselves, or do we need to acknowledge when something is no longer acceptable and therefore not expectable? By relieving ourselves from certain expectations, we can live the life we truly expect for ourselves.

Rummaging around, trying to find something sound?

Have you ever found yourself looking through things in different places and not finding what it is you're looking for? Have you ever found yourself looking in the fridge and kitchen cupboards and despite having lots of food, still finding it difficult to find what you really want? The same can be said for picking out clothes as well as what to do, where to go, and even what to say!

I have come to realise that sometimes we can be met with challenges when it comes to grasping what has true value and what has personal meaning and significance. Looking for something sound could reflect what we want from an interaction, experience, or even life, which is not always easy to identify. It could be something we are endlessly searching for, or it could be elicited by moments in our lives where we have encountered some kind of hardship or adversity and we need to fill a void.

Sometimes it can be relatively easy to recognise what we need and to identify ways of finding it. I believe self-care is what we all need, which undoubtedly will look different from one person to another and also at different times in a person's life. Equally important is the need to have something which creates meaning and purpose. For some this could be taking on certain roles and responsibilities, developing skills, strengths, and talents or engaging in interests and leisure pursuits. Regardless of what it is, I think it all comes down to the way we relate to ourselves and the world. Let's reflect on that for a moment. How do you find you relate to yourself? How do you find the way you relate to the world?

You may have found yourself deconstructing what it is you ultimately need and channelling that into the different pursuits and engagements you have in your life. Or maybe you haven't found what you are looking for, and seeing other people having found theirs, you feel under more pressure to find your thing, or whether there really is anything that you can claim and hold on to.

Let's go to a time when you did find something sound. It may or may not have been a recent time and you may not have recognised having found something significant at the time. Looking back now, what did it offer you? What role and impact did it have? Does a part of you want to re-connect with that moment and draw more from it so as to offer yourself something you believe you need in the present? If you find it difficult recalling such a moment, that's OK. It's also an invitation for you to explore, possibly coming across something you had not initially anticipated. This could become the very thing you need to make life that much sounder.

Life is a piece of cake

It is likely that you have come across the phrase, "It's a piece of cake," which communicates the efficiency, ease, and smoothness of achieving a desired outcome. But do we want everything to be that way? I imagine many of us would say, 'Of course, why make life any harder?' When it comes to making a cake, there are different ingredients, steps, and actions which are needed to make it. It may seem easy, but there are procedures that go into producing a cake.

Drawing parallels between a cake and life, the way a cake is divided into sections, so can our time, attention, and resources. Furthermore, when it comes to life, we need to piece together factors which can bring about positivity, and combine what is necessary, meaningful, and fulfilling.

A cake needs different ingredients in different quantities and in different proportions to one another. It needs to be baked at the right temperature and for a specific length of time to produce the desired texture, consistency, and physical appearance we would like it to have. Let's start with the basics. Flour is usually the main ingredient when it comes to making a cake, which provides the structure and the foundation for holding the other ingredients together.

Regarding life, I imagine each of us has some kind of "flour" that we find fundamental, which can be things like our relationships, job, hobbies, or place in the community. With both making a cake as well as life, things are needed to provide structure, add flavour, and promote growth. Relatedly, there may be times in our lives when, just like a cake, we add various ingredients in different quantities, some which complement each other and others which we may find unappealing and unappetising.

Akin to the layers of a cake, life can also involve different stages and having some kind of base can enable us to move to another place or "layer" with more stability. There might be times where certain parts need to be worked on separately, requiring different processes, stages, and timeframes. There may also be times where you will need to step back and wait for a part to form, develop, and mature.

Seeing life as a tiered cake where we need to spend different amounts of time and attention as well as utilising different resources can at times set off doubt, frustration, and tension. What's more is that we may try with great strife to make life as presentable as possible, where from the outside it may appear "perfect". We may present our lives and ourselves in the way we want others to see it and us or believe we need to show.

What we fundamentally need is to show ourselves that there is abundance and variety when it comes to what we can add to our lives and give it the substance and richness it needs to make it that much more appealing.

See you, be you

Let me ask you this; when was the last time you looked at yourself in the mirror? When you did, what did you see? How did you look at yourself? Is what you saw what you also see when you look at yourself at a deeper level? I am aware that it can be a challenge for us to really see what we want to in ourselves. I imagine most people have heard of the terms "putting on a brave face", "painting on a smile", "turning that frown upside down", and "putting on a mask", yet how much of ourselves is authentic if we are attempting to be seen in a certain way? I can anticipate that there may be times when it is not completely possible for all of what we are to be seen, especially if being totally genuine with ourselves may require some sort of support which is not available at the time or in the place we are in.

Let me paint a picture for you. Imagine a time when you have felt so sad that you believed all you needed to do was to talk to someone, to anyone. It could be a complete stranger whom you talk to as you're waiting for a bus, or picking up the phone and calling a helpline. It could also be that you have a support network of different individuals who you can approach and talk to about different issues.

My clients say how much of a relief it is for them to talk to me as someone who is impartial and who doesn't judge them or expect anything from them. It is a place where they can develop a more authentic relationship with themselves, where they feel seen and can subsequently see more of themselves. Through seeing more of oneself, a person can better understand themself and what they need. Sometimes these can be sourced from quite simple things, and at other times, it may require more attention and direction. Personally speaking, having an unfiltered conversation with a friend can make me feel so much at ease with and in myself. Another time it can be going for a walk to get some clarity and space as well as some grounding to retune myself. Sometimes just unwinding after a tough day and looking forward to a nice meal is all I need, and possibly other tools and resources I have written about in this section of the book. What we need and the amount we need such things can vary, though we need an ongoing commitment and investment in self-care. I now invite you to ask yourselves this: what are the places you can find yourself in? In such places, what do you see when you see you? I wholeheartedly hope it is a reflection of how you truly need to be, a moment where you are your authentic self.

Being our imperfect, perfect selves.

'That's perfect!' 'I didn't get it perfect.' 'It needs to be perfect.' 'I'm not perfect!' I am pretty sure that many of us have encountered such assertions.

Getting things perfect, getting things right, exceeding expectation, excelling, and achieving highly in every pursuit can seem impossible. Doing things perfectly would in many ways reflect that we are perfect beings, free from flaw. Striving for "perfection" can be a reflection of us trying to remove aspects of ourselves which are not fitting and in some ways do not seem right, fair, or just. In addition, aiming to be "perfect" can become a defence for us believing, we are untouched by different events, encounters, and experiences. It can create a barrier in being how we how we express or be ourselves. If we could be perfect, would that mean that life would also be perfect? Where all would be just right and there would be nothing to interfere with the harmony; nothing causing threat, pain, or distress. Well, I imagine that would be an ideal for many of us, yet the reality can seem far from it. Although it may lead to dishearten and disappointment, perfection can never really be something that is ever possible. At the end of the day, we are all human and therefore need to treat ourselves and each other with compassion.

If we are to have some kind of affiliation with the concept of perfection, it may be more regarding acknowledging, embracing, and understanding the inevitable dilemmas, disappointments, and let downs we are likely to face and may be playing some part in. It is about being accepting and embracing that reality, seeing the whole of ourselves and the entirety of our lives.

It is by being more accepting of all of ourselves that is ultimately the "perfect" way of being, enabling us to perfectly be ourselves.

To all my readers, wherever you are, I would like to thank you for deciding to read my book, to navigate its content, journey, and destination, allowing yourself to relate to and connect with another and possibly with yourself. I trust the process will lead to you reflecting on how your life has come to be and how we all have a story to tell. Life may not be "perfect" or may not pan out the way we hoped it would, yet we can free ourselves from the confined view or narrative we may have created. It is through acknowledging, being attentive and responsive to ourselves where we can triumph. It is this way of relating to ourselves, others, and the world that can lead to us moving from a defeated position to one where we are being defeating.